HEALING LANDSCAPES

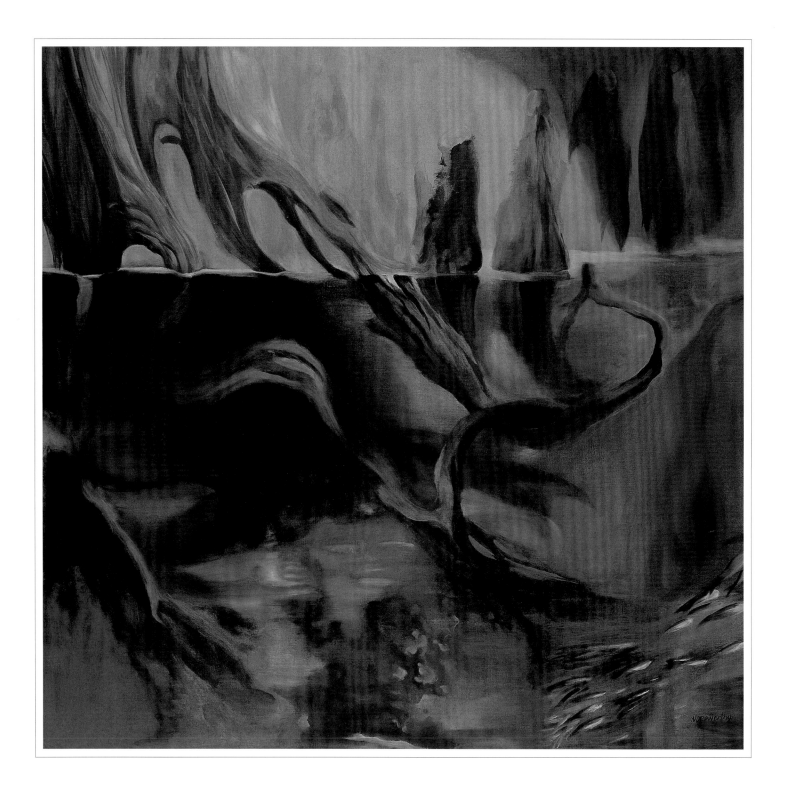

Healing Landscapes

A JOURNEY FROM THE BIG THICKET TO THE BIG BEND

Jeanne Norsworthy

Forewords by Geraldine Watson & David Alloway

Epilogue by Susan Hallsten McGarry

TEXAS A&M UNIVERSITY PRESS • COLLEGE STATION

LIBRARY OF CONGRESS CATALOGING-IN-PUBLICATION DATA

Norsworthy, Jeanne, 1935–1998
   Healing landscapes : a journey from the Big Thicket to the
   Big Bend / Jeanne Norsworthy ; forewords by Geraldine Watson,
   David Alloway ; epilogue by Susan Hallsten McGarry—1st ed.
      p. cm.— (Joe and Betty Moore Texas art series ; no. 11)
   ISBN 1-58544-140-6(alk. paper)
   1. Norsworthy, Jeanne, 1935-1998. 2. Artists—United States—
   Texas—Biography. 3. Big Thicket (Tex.)—In art. 4. Big Bend
   Region (Tex.)—In art. I. Title. II Series.
   ND237.N5995 A2 2001
   759.13—dc21   2001001895

My gift,

with love and gratitude,

to my six Rutherford children:

Patrick, Maidie, Paul, David, Stevan, & Kathryn

CONTENTS

ix   List of Illustrations

xi   Foreword, "Peace for the Big Thicket," by Geraldine Watson

xiii   Foreword, "The Spiritual Essence of Big Bend," by David Alloway

xv   Preface

3   Introduction

7   CHAPTER 1   *Spirit Bird Speaks*

37   CHAPTER 2   *Call of the Desert*

61   CHAPTER 3   *Siren Night Song*

81   CHAPTER 4   *Letting Go*

103   Epilogue, by Susan Hallsten McGarry

ILLUSTRATIONS

DRAWINGS

Tree trunk patterns, page 7

Flower sketches, 9

Palmetto forest, 10

Carnivorous pitcher plants, 11

Magnolia tree, 14

Survivor magnolia tree, 15

Cypress swamp and water tupelo, 17

The Easons, son and his wife, 20

The Easons, grandchild and Eason sons, 21

Long draw, 37

Blair Pittman, 38

Arch, Badlands, Lajitas, 45

Clay hills, 46

Owls and others, 61

Western side of Solitario, 62

Roadrunner, 73

Great wall of Chihuahua, 81

Longhorns-Rancho Picachos, 83

PLATES

1. *Village Creek Crowd*, page xii

2. *My Morning View*, xiv

3. *Cypress Creek Swamp*, 5

4. *Magnolia*, 13

5. *Lament the Lost Forest*, 16

6. *Steinhagan Lake*, 19

7. *Wolf Creek and Spider Lilies*, 23

8. *Honey Island*, 25

9. *Pink Rookery at Sunset*, 27

10. *Catfish Slough*, 29

11. *Life and Death of the Magnolia* series, 30-33

12. *Temples and the Parkway*, 34

13. *Can You Get to Heaven on a Flat Tire?*, 36

14. *Storm over Terlingua*, 41

15. *Red Bow over Reed Plateau*, 43

16. *Clay Hills with Indian Banding*, 44

17. *Abandoned Uranium Mine*, 48

18. *Morning Sun on Poster Peak*, 51

19. *Canyon de las Brujas*, 53

20. *Rain at Rancho Saus*, 54

21. *Backlit Leatherstem*, 57

22. *Carlotta Tinaja*, 58

23. *This Land Is My Land*, 65

24. *Women's Ancient Mysteries*, 67

25. *Love Song from Mexico*, 68

26. *Reading* Newsweek, 70

27. *Century Plant in Bloom*, 72

28. *The Man Who Sleeps in Cactus*, 74

29. *The Mating Dance of the Yucca Moth*, 76

30. *Canopus in Winter Sky*, 78

31. *Shaman Summoning My Broken Spirit*, 84

32. *Northern Lights*, 86

33. *Cactus and Cloud Streets*, 89

34. *The Shaman's Circle of Self*, 91

35. *The West Door*, 92

36. *Releasing My Eagles*, 94

37. *The Spirit of the Rio Grande*, 96

38. *Detaching: Flight of the Poppies #2*, 99

Foreword

PEACE FOR THE BIG THICKET

by Geraldine Watson

Once, I read an article in a magazine about an experiment to determine the effects of nature on mental patients. These severely ill people were moved from cells of an institution to a pleasant, airy building with a veranda on a mountainside overlooking a panorama of sky, snow-capped peaks, lake, and forest. A woman who had been in a catatonic state for thirty years sat surveying the scene and spoke the words, "Ah! Peace!"

In Jeanne Norsworthy's paintings, I see a soul in the process of escaping from walls built of physical, spiritual, and emotional pain—walls as debilitating as those of a prison cell. But one day a door opened, and she escaped into a garden where the sounds of nature stole into her mind and spirit, expelling her crippling fears, anxieties, and pain. A squirrel scampering along a limb, birds in a magnolia tree, the whispering breeze, and shimmering beams of sunlight through the leaves replaced tranquilizers, painkillers, and sleeping pills. Through this open door, Jeanne entered the natural world and began to search for healing scenes and sounds that she could place on canvas and share with others who are, as she had been, in dire need of peace.

From the dark waters of slough and stream in the Big Thicket rise the pure white crinum lily, the towering cypress pointing to a plane flying high above the mud and murky water, and the wings of water birds reaching for the freedom of the skies. The healing power of these earth elements inspired Jeanne to become an activist. Through depicting them, she attempts to slow if not halt the juggernaut of "progress" and salvage remnants of this planet as it was, created by an omniscient Deity who designed and installed upon it a system in perfect balance and harmony. When He decided the habitat was most ideal, He placed humans here with the admonition to "dress it and keep it."

Those who have lived as long as Jeanne and I have watched the "Edens" of our youth devastated and made hideous because of human greed and avarice. The gentle, undulating fields of grasses and wildflowers have become flat, hard surfaces of concrete and asphalt or neat rows of crops carefully controlled by chemicals. Hills are leveled, valleys filled, shrubs neatly clipped, and the soothing curves of the natural scene replaced by the sharp angles of cities. Everything has to be straight and level, vertical and horizontal.

We realize we cannot halt "progress" in this culture.

So we are doing what we can to restore and protect the balance of nature in our own small corner of this world, making it available to all who need a sanctuary in which to hide and lick their wounds—to preserve its healing scenes on canvas, in words, and in books such as this.

—*Geraldine Watson*

PLATE I. *Village Creek Crowd, n.d., oil, 40" x 50"*

Foreword

THE SPIRITUAL ESSENCE OF BIG BEND

by David Alloway

Geographically speaking, the Big Bend of Texas is defined as a redirection of the Rio Grande, taking a long detour into the Chihuahuan Desert on its way to the Gulf of Mexico. Nestled in the crook of the river's southern dip is a land of high-forested mountains, deep canyons, and long desert flats. Its flora and fauna are said to be more representative of Mexico than the United States, and "diverse" is perhaps the most used adjective to describe the region.

However, the Big Bend is more than a consequence of topography. It represents a vision often brought to mind at the mention of Texas. The Big Bend is Texas lost in time. This region evokes a sense of frontier and brings out primal emotions. Like the land, its people are a special lot. Many of us are refugees from the rushed chaos of urban life. Viewed by outsiders as anachronisms, we see ourselves as independent, with little use for sociological problems that are attached to the conveniences of civilization. The river is also an international boundary—a fact largely ignored by citizens living on either side. Few borders are as peaceful and friendly.

The wild beauty and freedom of the Big Bend offers a spirituality as diverse as its land and people. Few encounter the Big Bend without some inner experience, and those who do not are usually the type of person whose soul has long departed and whose body forgot to quit breathing. It is sometimes hard to express the spiritual attachment of the Big Bend, but Jeanne broke this barrier not only with her art but also with the way she touched those who knew her.

Artists and photographers lured to the Big Bend to "capture" its majestic scenery are often disappointed to find their work loses its openness when framed or bordered. Jeanne's paintings, however, are not limited by the height or width of her canvas. What defines her art is *depth*. To see Jeanne's work is to experience the spiritual Big Bend. What other explanation is there for a flat surface of canvas and pigment allowing one to step inside and look around? Like her subject, Jeanne's art goes beyond the measure of dimension. This is because she painted not only with brushes but also with natural spirituality. Those who knew Jeanne, and those who view her art, are seeing the Big Bend through her soul.

I was a foreman of Fresno Ranch when Jeanne and David Sleeper were still married. Her candor and subsequent divorce grieved me, but I rejoiced in the subsequent healing and how she expressed it in this book. While the way I practice my spirituality may be different from Jeanne, we shared common bonds. When we would meet and hug as friends do, I was touched by her heart. When I look at her work, now that she is gone, I still feel the wondrous healing. I know the paintings within this book will share those feelings with you as well.

—David Alloway

PLATE 2.
My Morning View, 1985, oil, 40" x 40"

PREFACE

My earliest role model was my grandmother, Maidie Dealey Moroney, whom I called Bunny. I saw her sit in her farm neighbors' shacks, which stunk of mildew, stale tobacco, kerosene, and who knows what else. While the old man and the old woman talked, toothless, and spat in an old Folgers coffee can, Bunny refused to show the slightest sign of disgust.

Although they were chewing tobacco and spitting constantly, my grandmother chatted with them on an equal level as peers. Then she would drive back into Dallas, where we both lived, and dress for a cocktail party she was giving for Clare Booth Luce, the ambassador to Italy and wife of Time/Life owner Henry Luce.

She was always generous to others, frequently over-tipping waiters and whispering to me, "They need it more than I do." The next day she was out on the farm again, driving a tractor, wearing a plaid jacket and a baseball cap. My grandmother could walk with beggars or kings. She never changed her demeanor but treated all people with courtesy and respect, displaying her delightful sense of humor (especially when the joke was on her).

While sharing the lives of the I. C. Eason family, spending weekends in their river shack with them or in their small home in Silsbee, I had my chance to really try to live up to my grandmother's example. I had been married to a multimillionaire oilman, whom I divorced after fifteen years and six children, and I still lived in prestigious River Oaks. The divorce settlement and my own family's wealth put me up in that class where one might be expected to act superior.

I owe a huge debt of gratitude to the Easons, for I could never have known the Big Thicket as I came to know it without their stories and without them personally guiding me around the area. I had always found haughty, stuck-up people to be a huge bore and naturally gravitated toward anyone who was real and honest. I had my convictions borne out by the Easons' love and loyalty. I needed that "reality check," and these wonderful people took me in as part of their family, not knowing for months the full truth of my "other" lifestyle. It was like traveling incognito and soothing to my rich woman's suspicions that some people only liked me for my position. The Easons, so different from me but so similar in other ways, prepared me for the glorious eccentricities of the community of the Big Bend. I hope my neighbors also consider me as wonderfully eccentric as I see them to be, each in his or her own way.

I also owe a debt of gratitude to Blair Pittman, whom I married after five years of living single with my brood of mostly teenagers. His thirty-page article on the Big Thicket for the *National Geographic Magazine* gave him renown, and his pictures were often published in the *Houston Chronicle.* He not only introduced me to the Easons but also to the Big Bend and to my final husband, David Sleeper. I have had enough adventures for several lifetimes, and through all these I have discovered my own inner strength, inner guidance, and the ability to trust myself. I have gone from oilman husband to photographer and book-writer husband to penniless ranch-owner husband. I adore my single life, believing I have "paid my dues" and earned it!

HEALING LANDSCAPES

INTRODUCTION

If you are in turmoil,

discover the renewal

you will get

in a walk

around the block.

ONE DAY WHEN I WAS DESPERATE OVER the effects of chemotherapy and the craziness that the large doses of cortisone gave me, I went outdoors in the enclosed yard of my small house in Houston. There was no conscious plan except that I possibly could find release outdoors. I took a book by Larry Dossey on prayer, read a page, then sat and watched the squirrels and birds in my magnolia tree. I read another page and prayed about healing. My dogs lay quietly nearby, sensing that today was different; they must not bark or chase squirrels.

As the dogs stretched out on the decking, I fell inwardly silent and somehow became part of the world. It was no longer little me going through hard times. I no longer prayed but became the prayer. The sun was setting and the amber lights from the Galleria colored the twilight clouds apricot, which although artificial was beautiful against the dark navy sky. Before I knew it I had been sitting quietly for five or six hours—something impossible the last few months because of the cortisone. I went indoors at last, filled with peace and calm. I slept without a sleeping pill for the first time in months, and the cortisone I continued to take never affected me again.

I believe we can effectively alter the way our bodies respond to all things. We may not know, nor did I realize before that miraculous day, how connecting to God, nature, and all things could bring me such joy and healing. I had no idea that the effect could last months. I took cortisone in massive doses thereafter with no unpleasant side effects.

Although I have always been aware of the healing power of nature, that day in my backyard confirmed that I did not have to take a trip to get to nature. We live in it; we are part of it. The DNA in our bodies is also in every living tree, grass, flower, and animal, only the coding varies. We are all one.

Unfortunately, we have, as a society, become so removed from the natural life of the outdoors that many people I know experience fear whenever they set foot in the woods or in the desert. They cannot believe that "things" are not going to leap out and bite or attack them. Yet I have wandered across the desert for years, slept in my bedroll on the ground, and nothing has bitten or attacked me. I walk through tall grasses at my ranch in Bellville and wander barefoot through my spring-fed creeks. If there is a snake, I give it time to move away and then continue on my way; it does not desire to eat a human, nor bite one, nor even come close to one. Snakes, and other creatures, have a right to be here as much as I do.

Many people have lost the ability to go into nature to experience the healing that awaits them there. But I can promise that merely sitting on a park bench, watching life flowing by, and becoming quiet inside can produce more than one ever dreamed possible. Even the civilized city parks can provide that kind of sanctuary a person inexperienced in the wilds so desperately needs.

We could easily sink into desperation if we ponder not only our individual but also our world environment. How can we heal ourselves if we succumb to greed, killing species of plants we could have used for the cure of many horrible diseases? How can we piously stand in church knowing that every minute thousands of acres of rain forest are being destroyed? Don't we know something sacred is being desecrated? What can *we* do to heal this planet, our polluted home that holds so many answers for us? It contains as many plants to cure us as it holds viruses and bacteria to kill us. How can we find and experiment with them if we destroy them before we even know of their existence? Our home, Earth, may still contain clean air to breathe, clean water to drink, and unravaged forests. But if so, where, and for how much longer? I feel a certain powerlessness but also a sustaining hope that I could make a difference. That is why I wrote this book: to share my thoughts on two healing landscapes that are being destroyed as I write. The Big Thicket and Big Bend are two wildly different parts of Texas. Both have become themes of healing in my life and my art.

To the east is the Big Thicket, on the edge of the Louisiana border. It has seven ecological sections, often intermingled, that sometimes include plants and trees that only grow on the far eastern side of the Mississippi River. In my studio I recall the pine forests, the trees (beech, water tupelo, and cypress), the bogs, the swamp waters colored wine-red by the tannic acid of leaves, the flat prairies, the orchids, the carnivorous plants, the azaleas' delicate fragrance, and the wild abandon of wildflowers in the spring and summer. Even as I stretched a canvas to paint them I knew clear-cutting was taking place in the Thicket. I painted many of the trees transparent to indicate they may be gone even before I returned.

I was lucky enough to be able to spend six years in

PLATE 3. *Cypress Creek Swamp, 1979, oil, 24" x 36"*

the Big Thicket and see it before the area became a public commodity. I have mixed feelings about that fragile place. I want everyone to see it, but the public as a whole cannot be trusted: either children trample orchids or someone decides to dig one up, never understanding they will not transplant. So now the Thicket has designated trails, covered with wood chips, that one must follow. But the secret places are still open to those who are not afraid of getting lost.

To the west, Big Bend was another matter altogether. I lived there ten years and saw the desert in all her guises. By day she is strong, demanding, imposing, hard, spiny, powerful, and unrelenting. But to really understand Big Bend's beauty, one must meet her at night and see her magical softness, her indigo skies filled with stars.

I found myself using a different style to capture the beauty I found there. The desert presents itself as an indomitable area, one that demands adjustments by humans who wish to live there. But its fierce beauty is misleading. Underneath its vast façade, the desert is as fragile as orchids and ferns, more so because there is no more than an average of eight inches of rainfall annually, so damage done to its terrain is not repaired by water.

The plants and animals that can be reached by tourists are almost beyond restoration. Other people are cooking up schemes to get rich off the desert by pumping what underground water is left for building developments, indifferent to the fact of how slow the area's drinking water is replenished. Indifference has also destroyed irreplaceable archeological sites, and gravel mining in Terlingua Creek is destroying its channel. Meanwhile, the landscape is forever altered, flattened, and then abandoned like a woman despised, raped, and left for dead.

Many of my paintings of the Big Bend country speak of the region as it once was and still is in its unreachable areas. I have ridden as long as eleven hours roundtrip by horseback to get to the untouched wilderness, both in the Big Bend and in Mexico, to sketch it, photograph it, and bring it to my paintings. I hope these images encourage others to value, cherish, and do what they can to protect our precious planet. People must have beautiful wilderness for escape and in which to find sanctity. To soothe our wounds we must repair those people have made in nature. Healing begins when we project beyond ourselves to the global village in which we live and to the earth that nurtures it.

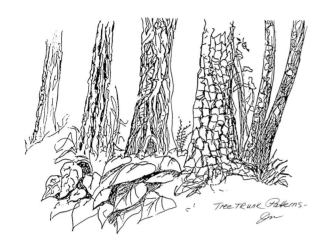

Tree Trunk Patterns—

Chapter 1

SPIRIT BIRD SPEAKS

My childish prayer

on my fourth birthday

was, "Dear God,

please make a bird,

any bird,

come and sit

on my shoulder."

I WAS ABOUT SIX OR SEVEN YEARS OLD when I first experienced feeling different, happier, and more whole. It came to me as I sat in a live oak tree.

The adults were visiting my great-grandmother, and their talk was boring. The live oak was fascinating. It was huge, but I climbed up to a smaller branch so I could feel it sway in the breeze. I was entranced into stillness, and a family of blue jays ignored me, perching on a branch nearby. I still get that old feeling of peace and serenity, acceptance and belonging, when I hear the call of the blue jay or feel a breeze on my face.

Years later, as karma goes, my daughter Maidie brought home a baby bird in a paper sack, a ball of gray fluff with a black ring around its neck, still with its egg beak. We were not even sure of its species.

The bird was too young to save, but by a miracle it lived and grew into a beautiful blue jay that adored me and sat on my shoulder as I watched television in the evenings. Ratting up my long hair, just like one does with a brush, the jay would settle in, hide, and make the bird equivalent of a purr. Only his tail would peek out, and after six children I knew enough to keep an extra diaper on my shoulder for droppings.

I named him/her Sammy Jay, and that precious bird considered me mama, during mating season, lover. A man who ran a bird shop said I could tell my bird's sex by holding it upside down in my hand and then blowing back the tummy feathers—if it is big, it is a boy, and if it is small, it is a girl. Big or small compared to what? I never knew. Sammy Jay spoke many English words such as "mother," "shoe," and "right now"; he also imitated the squeal of the refrigerator door being opened and sang in the mornings. After all the children were bundled off to school, the dishwasher started, and the coffee pot turned on, Sammy would begin to chortle, then whistle and sing like a canary. If I walked around the corner to watch him, though, he would act embarrassed and quit. Sammy also had a full repertoire of jay sounds, one of which he taught me. There were one or two people he hated, since they had once teased him. He would grasp his perch and let out a loud rattle while bobbing up and down. I thought the action was his own invention until one day, as I lay on my back beside Buffalo Bayou, a blue jay dropped to a branch near me, glared, and did the pump and rattle. I was obviously trespassing his area. The birds did not do that in my yard, though, because they accepted that I belonged there too.

Sammy Jay lived to be twelve years old and died on Mother's Day. Because the blue jay has been a spirit bird for me since my early childhood experience, I felt blessed to have the gift of his presence for so long, opening my eyes to another world.

I became a birder in my late twenties when I turned a pair of binoculars on a black bird sipping water from Onion Creek in central Texas. It turned out to have a blue head, a green back, and a bright red stomach. None of the colors were evident without the exact lighting or the binoculars; I later learned it was a painted bunting, one of the most glorious birds in the United States.

I spent the rest of the day in wonder, seeing all the dark, drab brown birds become not sparrows but warblers with yellow markings or white patterns or blue birds. I saw a russet brown thrush digging beneath a tree, knocking away leaves to get at the bugs underneath. Although I was struggling with a troubled marriage and difficulties with the children, this marvelous bird world was a delight that sustained me then and ever after. I could soon spot birds and identify them and their songs. When I sat in my backyard, watching the beautiful birds and listening to their songs, I gained greater perspective on my tiny life in this great world. There is beauty and life going on all around us, and though I am not the center of it, I belong.

The joy of discovery, the delight in nature's beauty so restored my soul, worn out from carpooling my brood of six children, homework, and teenage arguments, that I cherished the spiritual renewal I received even in my backyard. In small ways I began to receive additional solace there and to find with amazement the variety of birds, including three little screech owls, two coppery tailed trogons, a golden eagle escaped from the zoo, an indigo bunting, Mississippi kites, and redwing blackbirds, not to mention the usual thrushes, warblers, jays, cardinals, and sparrows.

I began to teach my children to sit outdoors and pretend they were blind, simply listen and feel the twilight give way to dusk. First, as the sun sets, a new breeze comes up, fresh and cool. The cicadas begin to sing with new power. With open eyes one sees the pink sunset paint the yard, making the green look greener. Purple creeps across the sky. Then there is stillness. The breeze ceases. The cicadas are silent. From a corner of the yard a green tree frog peeps: *Beep, bop, beep beep, bop bop.* Another tree frog responds from some other corner. Then the night breeze twirls around face and legs, and evening is here.

Flowers are so female.

No matter that they carry

male parts as well.

I would want to be as lovely as a flower

and as powerful in my womanliness.

AS I BECAME A REAL NATURALIST, EVERY flower became a new world under my camera's macro lens. The trees began to separate out, and I learned their names and began to know their bark patterns. I learned about the wild flowers, the grasses, then the stars, and the constellations. Wherever I went I tried to learn about the soil and the geology.

I began to see how nature had worked out ecological pockets that if disturbed destroyed many if not all of the special plants and animals. I talked to old-timers who remembered the natural state of the prairies and the woods, folks who had been young in the 1800s. I asked Dorothy Kuykendahl Hoskins, who had a ranch in Buda, Texas, on Onion Creek, to tell me about the places that looked like they had been carved out by springs but were now dry. She declared: "Why they were springs! There were springs gushing out everywhere until folks began pumping out the ground water, then those springs dried up. In our first years there weren't all these cedar trees, but grasses as high as a horse's belly. It gave good cover for the Indians as they snuck up on unsuspecting settlers. The only trees were these huge live oaks, and not that many of them." She told me how her mama had built their log cabin, which is now in a historical plot in

Dripping Springs. Dorothy told how they had plowed a field for food and how they could drink any water they came across, be it creek, river, or stream. The circle of stones I had seen from horseback, she mentioned, was an old meeting place for the Indians who gathered every fall for a huge reunion of families and hunting parties. Then came the ranchers with their cows and fences, and the grasses went, the cedars moved in to cover much of the land, the springs dried up, and Dorothy and her family adapted to each change.

The damp, the humidity

that one pushes through

as one pushes through bushes.

I have one son, Paul, who validates me.

He adores humidity,

as I also strangely do.

Returning from the desert

I suck in deep breaths of Houston,

of the Big Thicket, the sweet

taste of foliage in the air.

WHEN I FIRST HEARD THE BIG THICKET described, it sounded like a lot of hype to me. So in 1972 I joined a nature class to go as a group to see this place, only a hundred miles east of my Houston home. There were rumors that the Thicket held seven ecological areas, all woven together; one walked from cactus and sand into pine trees, flower-strewn prairies, and finally bogs of floating peat with orchids, carnivorous plants, and the like. I could not imagine how that might look or how it could have come about. If the Thicket were anything close to what I fantasized, it would be wonderful.

Geraldine Watson led the tour, and, I was to realize later, she had been a champion of the Big Thicket long before it became the center of a public controversy over how to save this unique area. My group boarded a bus in Houston and began the two-hour drive.

Palmetto forest
with Geraldine Watson —

The first stop, near Saratoga, was on the side of the highway, and the group, lots of little old ladies in tennis shoes and me, unloaded. I was just a kid then, in my late thirties. Geraldine led us to a barbed-wire fence, still talking, and clearly she expected everyone to climb over or crawl under just as she did. Some did not make it, and at this point, there was nothing to make you want to crawl anywhere, just deep woods. I figured I was being a good sport by going along with the plan.

We took a short walk under the trees. Nothing very unusual until suddenly we were in a palmetto flat, where the palmettos towered over us and hid us from each other. We had to negotiate how and where we would stand to even hear or see Geraldine. I still have photographs of that day: just straw hats here and there, their wearers obscured by giant tropical-looking palmettos, and Geraldine herself, with her long salt-and-pepper hair naturally beautiful, standing there perfectly at home.

We went to prairies and counted hundreds of species of flowers in bloom. Most of the varieties were new to me. I decided that this must be what all the fuss was about. Then we continued on to a bog where the rose pogonia orchid was blooming amidst the drooping flowers of carnivorous pitcher plants, just as I had been told of but could not believe until now. Shrubs of fragrant wax myrtle grew large. Their berries, I learned, were once used by pioneers to make bayberry candles. I was beginning to get the sense of the place. There really were amazing areas here, wildly different from each other, with wonderful flowers and trees everywhere.

Carniverous Pitcher Plants with flowers —

Like the mixture of races in America,

the upper story of trees mix their leaves,

a blend that is almost undecipherable.

As confusing as an Oriental-eyed woman

who speaks with a thick Spanish accent,

the trees pretend to conceal themselves.

I look up, hopelessly confused, yet thrilled by

the variety,

the mix of branches, in a puzzle of lines that

defies tracing to a tree trunk.

So now I must learn the pattern of tree trunks.

So now I must also learn the pattern of my

own

confused roots and the style of my own family.

A FEW YEARS LATER, AFTER I HAD BEEN exploring the Thicket every way I could, I attended an annual weekend gathering in Saratoga with my brother, George. We had bedrolls, two little tents, Coleman stove, coffeepot (essential), and a little grill. We got some snack foods at a little store near Rye, Texas, and camped by a stream. We were signed up for walking tours for the next two days.

I had learned from talking to the locals that mysterious and dangerous things had been going on in the depths of the Thicket recently, responses to the controversy caused by the government taking over privately held land, timberland, ponds, and bogs. The "nature lovers" wanted too much, the charge went. Folks who had lived there for generations began to resort to destructive tactics. Certain businesses, like timbering, may have even banded together with the locals. Vandalism and devastation of prime areas of the Big Thicket had begun. If it was ruined, some thought, then maybe the "park folks" will give up.

Even a few recent deaths were rumored to be murders, not accidents. For instance, a driver in a car wreck, a teetotaler, was found with alcohol poured over his clothes and a bullet in the back of his head; the death had been ruled accidental. The victim, coincidentally, had been fighting to help create the national park. In other cases, missing persons were never found; the bogs go deep.

I was nervous then and glad to have a guide. In those days you did not want to be found trespassing on anyone's land.

One tour was especially amazing. By that time the Big Thicket National Park was underway, and a ranger was going to lead us. It just so happened that the area of the Neches River bottom we were going to see had

PLATE 4.
Magnolia, 1977, oil,
48" x 36"

recently flooded. "I think we can go on anyway, if y'all don't mind getting a little wet," the ranger told us.

Everyone on the tour agreed to go. We drove in caravans to the end of a road and stopped to look at an ancient magnolia tree that had plants growing on its branches, just like you see on the huge live oaks in central Texas. The trunk was big enough for six men to circle holding hands.

We trudged down the road, seeing up ahead the swirling red waters. I was the only woman on the hike, consequently the shortest person, carrying two expensive cameras and wearing my favorite Redwing boots. The ranger said, "This is where we have to cross the flood waters and I'll go in first." Not one man said a word, but all followed eagerly. I stared at the faces around me and decided that I was willing to take this adventure too.

At first the water covered my ankles, but then rose to my knees. I carefully watched my brother, who is five feet, eight-inches tall, and noticed where the water came up on him. Next thing I knew we were at the confluence of some creek and the Neches River, and what there was of a road was probably gone. Water flowed in angles on my left and sometimes swirled in a circle; a whirlpool was only ten feet away. It looked deadly to me.

On the ranger plunged. One man did not walk exactly where our guide had and dropped off into water up to his chest; he was six feet tall. I began to mentally say goodbye to my cameras. If I dropped into such a hole, I would be in water up to my neck.

Privately, we each were hoping to be back on high ground soon. I carefully walked exactly where my brother did while holding my cameras up. As long as the water did not rise past his belt, I figured I could make it too. The waters turned out to be more extensive than the ranger anticipated (probably they were rising as we walked). We were able to see some champion trees and got a good feeling for floods. Eventually it became fun, hiking through those floodwaters for four hours! Never saw a snake or an alligator, but they would have been there in large numbers.

As our group returned, we reached dry land near the giant magnolia tree, a silent witness to centuries of floods and storms. Its magnificence touched me deeply, for it was more incredible than any of the champion trees we had spent four hours struggling to see.

That magnolia known for its great age and girth had a spread so fabulous that a plan was made to show it to some congressmen visiting the Big Thicket from Washington. If they saw the wonders of this place, hopefully, they would work to support plans for a national park.

The men arrived and were taken to see the tree, but as they approached the site, it was clear that the evergreen magnolia was dead. It had been healthy just the week before.

In time, an investigation proved the tree had been injected with cyanide in several places around its trunk. I never heard if the culprit was found.

PLATE 5. *Lament the Lost Forest, 1977, oil, 36" x 48"*

AFTER FIVE YEARS OF EXPLORING THE Big Thicket, I met a photographer named Blair Pittman at an annual gathering in Saratoga. He not only shared many of my interests, but we also knew some of the same people who were the "standard bearers" of the Thicket, like Harold Nicklaus, Archer Fullingim, Geraldine Watson, Bill Brett, and Bill's wife, Anna Lou.

Bill, who had written a book of local tall tales, impressed me with his wit and many talents. He had an on-going struggle with narcolepsy and talked freely about how disappointing it was to fear an attack of sudden deep sleep.

One day, Blair and I arrived as Bill was creating a rope of horsehair. He had a special rig on his fence, and as he turned a handle and fed horsehair from a large sack hung over his shoulder into the contraption while walking backward, rope began to form. After watching Bill for a time, I wanted to try it; he made it look so easy. Blair and I tried making a section—our piece of rope was thick, then thin, then rough, then scraggly. I had to admire Bill's skill. He also made nifty hatbands of chosen horsehair colors and has gone to the folk festival in San Antonio for many years to show off his crafts. When Bill makes fried apple pies, you are really lucky to be his guest.

Another time, when we were leaving his house at dusk, Bill suggested we stop and watch the snakes mating in the pools of rainwater by the curve of his road. We reached the spot and saw the water swirling strangely. Exiting the Jeep, we saw the orange western sky reflected off the bodies of at least two dozen cottonmouth snakes roiling a small four-by-ten-foot pool. Bodies continued to tumble like wash in a washer, a never-ending orgy of snakes. They did not pay any attention to our presence, nor did they seem to pause to come up for air.

Snakes were not a problem on any of the many hikes or campouts. The Thicket is rich in all forms of life, especially bird life. I enjoyed trekking into certain places kept secret by those who protect the area to watch for any sign of the near extinct ivory-billed woodpecker. We found the old cypress trees where the "last ones" had hollowed out their huge nest holes, high up and large enough for a big dog to crawl into. We studied chips on the ground below, hoping against hope that it was "sign," only to see a pileated woodpecker fly up to continue the excavation. We played tapes of the ivory-billed woodpecker's call. The ensuing silence answered a question I had been asking for a decade.

Cypress Swamp & water tupelo

I know that when

I touched my great-grandmother,

I touched the Civil War,

and Time,

Time before electricity

or cars.

I know that when I heard

the calls of the last ivory-billed woodpeckers,

I was standing on

the edge of another Age.

IN THE LATE 1960s, MY FIRST HUSBAND and our children took a drive to the Sam Houston State Forest near Cut-and-Shoot, Texas. We traveled down one red-dirt road after another, finally stopping to let the children run around a little. As the kids cavorted and screamed, "Watch this, Mother," I began to notice a strange tooting call and something that sounded like a carpenter building a house up in the treetops.

I had never in my life heard such a strange call from a bird, and the sound made the hair stand up on the back of my neck. I realized there were two huge birds, hidden in the treetops, hammering with impressive force and noise while calling to each other. I could not get anyone in the family to listen and wonder with me, so I began to walk off into the woods. The birds kept a few trees ahead of me, and always out of sight, too high above the tree canopy to glimpse them. I gave up after a while and returned to my family, saying that I had been hearing the most incredible birds. Who cared! Back into the car for more driving.

The first time I heard Bill Brett's tape of the ivory-billed woodpecker, I gasped and felt tears fill my eyes. I recognized that call! I had heard perhaps the last pair alive, and at the least I had been overwhelmed enough to never forget it.

Several other folks in the Thicket believed there were a few holdouts still alive in the untraveled depths of the forest. An ivory-bill easily could fly a hundred miles a day for food and required huge dead cypress trees for its nest. As the desire for prized cypress grew, the large trees were felled and dragged out of the forests and swamps. Then clear-cutting took over as the preferred practice, and whole areas of diverse ecologies were destroyed. All of this slowly wiped out the ivory-bills' food supply and nesting places, and the birds became extinct. We never heard or saw a sign of ivory-bills, but we talked to plenty of people who remember the last ivory-billed woodpecker they ever saw. They remembered the day, the weather, the exact tree, and the goose bumps those huge birds inspired in all who came near them.

Because bird life is rich in the Thicket, I would not dream of going there now without my best ten-power birding binoculars. And a "heard bird" is as good as a sighting.

PLATE 6. *Steinhagan Lake, 1979, oil, 28" x 36"*

The one hundred miles to the Easons

Took me back one hundred years.

I sensed how life was

for my pioneer ancestors.

Hardships brought the family closer

And a pang of envy seized me.

BLAIR PITTMAN INTRODUCED ME TO
many people in the Big Thicket, but best of all, he
introduced me to the Eason family, whose ancestors
came from Appalachia generations ago.

There is nothing gentle about the people who came
to the Thicket during the Civil War, seeking refuge in its
impenetrable centers. They have developed their own
system of justice based on what they value to be right
and wrong. Some might have been criminals; others just
did not want to fight in the Civil War. Their rules,
adapted from Appalachia in many cases, were fought over
amongst themselves to see who would come out on top.

I do not know all the details, but I can imagine that
I. C. Eason earned his title as King of the Dog People.
Sometimes he would tell some tales, and you would get a
whiff, like someone opening a cellar door, of a by-gone
age that may not be entirely over yet.

Later, as I would get to know the King of the Dog
People and his family, I counted myself lucky to be their
friend and to stay with them in the depths of forest they
considered their own. I was even able to return their

generosity by having them as houseguests in Houston.
We both experienced culture shock in each other's
homes, so opposite were our lifestyles. But we laughed
about it openly. It was a balm to my inner wound.
Because I was born well off, I felt an unwanted distance
between myself and others not so fortunate. Yet these
accepting people took me in with open arms, with a
sense of being equals.

I soon learned that visiting empty handed was never
done. The most appreciated gifts were a big can of
Folgers coffee and five pounds of sugar. There was always
a pot of coffee going, and when they would add to it
heaping spoonfuls of sugar, it was obvious why they were
glad I had brought more.

The dining area of the kitchen opened to the
backyard, and the goats there would wander in most of
the time, looking for handouts like a pet dog. There was

Eason Son

Billie, his wife

Daughter-in-law to I. C. Eason

Eason grandchild

Eason Sons

no screen door. We always sat in the kitchen and talked for hours. We would crowd together at the small lino-leum-topped table and the jawing would begin! The grown children who knew we were coming made it a point to show up too, and the family teased each other loudly and repeatedly, acting insulted, only to break out into deep laughter while adding an even better barb.

Sometimes one would start the lyrics to a song, which everyone would take up. The Easons listened to records and tapes of country music, and they could sound just like Johnny Cash and his family. They were really good.

Once when Lorine decided to cook some chickens for us all, I. C. stepped into the backyard, still talking, and grabbed a hen, whose squawking only made him talk louder. He returned, stood beside us at the table, began swinging the chicken by the head, and then slung it through the open door into the yard, where it flapped

and died suddenly. "No," they all assured me, "that thar hen were plumb gone from the first swing." The rest of the action was the reflex of a dead bird.

I sat there and relaxed carefully, knowing I was back in time to a place where death in order to eat was ordi-nary. Until now, all my chickens were sanitized and devoid of horror under clear wrap in a plastic tray. I slowly marveled at the reality of life and love here in these deep woods. After a while, Lorine went out back, collected the hen, and plucked it there. We ate well, that chicken boiled with onions along with a pan of Lorine's incredible three-inch-thick biscuits, which she stirred up without even thinking. These folks had lived off the land all their lives, growing collards, corn, and some other vegetables, but most of their food came from trapping or hunting.

I kept up my close friendship with the Easons, and we enjoyed laughing at the difference in our back-grounds, especially my ignorance of all the things they understood. Several times they came to Houston, and I. C. and Lorine stayed in my large house. They were perfectly relaxed and joked about getting lost in my home like I did in their Neches River bottom. But when I. C. saw the crystal chandelier in my entry hall, really a modest little fixture, he hollered for Lorine to come and see it. "Com' on here now, Lorine. They done got diamonds hanging from the ceiling!" He knew better, but he joked about the diamonds for the rest of the weekend. The next time I went to visit the Easons, they greeted me at the door and escorted me inside in a new formal way, grinning at each other. When I reached our usual chatting spot, the kitchen table, there over the table hung a crystal chandelier! Nevertheless, the back door was still open and the goat still came in when he pleased.

I learned of I. C.'s death with grief, and a few years afterward Lorine died. I feel the loss of those people.

What is more romantic

than lying in a tall bed of fern

while your husband looks deeply

into your eyes, then

bends to kiss you?

I AM SLOW TO PAINT A NEW LOCATION. Things get put on a back burner, to stew for a year or two before they are ready to go on canvas. Then one day I wake up and all I can think about is an idea that has been slipping around in the backwoods of my mind for a long time.

I did not want to be "just another painter of trees," as my Houston gallery dealer Meredith Long succinctly warned me. What was it about the Big Thicket that moved me? What was it that came up in my dreams, that made me want to return again and again despite mosquitoes, lengthy packing procedures, a two-hour drive just to get on the edge of the area, exhausting hikes all day, usually no real trails, bushwhacking through dense underbrush, and then a two-hour drive back?

It was the unexpected things I discovered that drew me back again and again, like the day we wandered into a place filled with thirty-inch-high cinnamon ferns. On another occasion, we unexpectedly came upon a bog. I thought I was just walking along on solid ground until I noticed a spring under my feet. The centuries of sphagnum moss created a surface that supported my weight, rocking underneath as I moved, much like walking on a waterbed. But there were moments when I suddenly sank up to my ankles or more and the water rushed up around my leg.

After I began my series on the Big Thicket, Geraldine Watson came to my house to visit. I showed her one of the paintings. She sank into a chair, sighed, and with tears in her eyes said, "This is the first time I've seen something that gets the feel of the Thicket, the way I feel about it." I could not ask for better praise from any better critic.

PLATE 7.
Wolf Creek
and Spider
Lilies, 1978, oil,
40" x 50"

Graceful pitcher plants,

their lily-like flowers drooping,

some reddened by winter,

others green and yellow,

so innocently they stand,

filled inside their tubular stems

with insects, even a lizard

whom you'd expect to know better.

Oh, so charmingly have men beckoned me.

I too have been curled up,

disintegrating in a trap of sweet lies.

THERE IS A LITTLE SPOT, MAYBE BIG enough to be called a town, that I pass on the way to Silsbee. I had stopped one day on the side of the highway to check for spring flowers and found a stream. On its banks were three species of violets, iridescent green moss, and tall ferns. I began to stop here frequently and watched the change of the seasons' flowers.

One day I rounded the bend of the road preparing to stop and the place was gone. I thought I was mistaken. Maybe I had been daydreaming and had passed it already. But after turning around several times, I realized that this newly clear-cut field was the place, my place, where the violets and moss and fern grew, where the spider lilies spread out their fragrance in summer and grew with iris in the water.

All around lay desolation. Dogwoods lay like trash. Magnolia trees had fallen into the pile of their huge glossy leaves. Ash and oak had been bulldozed aside under hills of red dirt, and drag trails showed things had been pulled out.

The only trees that had any value for the clear-cut man was the pine, the incredible longleaf pine that takes many, many years just to set its tap root before it even grows a foot tall. I stood in the ruins and heard birds fly back and forth, knowing some must be searching for the tree that was their home. I thought of the animals that made this woods part of their territory and wondered how many had been inadvertently killed by the slaughter of the trees.

That day I went back to Houston, filled with sorrow and anger. In mourning for the loss, I began this painting. I recalled the beauty that was gone and that which still remained. I began to paint the trees as transparent because they were leaving, destined to be destroyed to provide some quick cash for someone. I had heard of the irreparable damage done by clear-cutting, but never had it hit home so deeply as when it happened to a place I treasured. Since some people have gotten away with doing this to whole populations of other people (genocide), trees do not stand a chance.

A year later, my place was planted in sweet little rows of "genetically upgraded" loblolly pine. No diversity, no wild understory of fragrant azalea, no vines of begonia and trumpet flower. Nowhere for the birds or animals to live that needed this variety of things. Creatures depend on the mix of grasses, bushes, flowers, seeds, and large and small trees of all kinds to round out their diet and provide habitat. Animals cannot live in rows of identical trees, nor can people survive in a cement-slab world. But there it was, just plowed and planted like tenement-row housing, all the same and just as barren.

This painting is both protest and gratitude. Gratitude for the active, politically minded folks who gave most of their lifetimes to saving what they could of this precious pocket of nature, this string of pearls in Texas.

I keep this painting hanging in my living room so I can recall my little place of splendor that did not even have a real name. For me, the name was Delight.

PLATE 8. *Honey Island, 1977, oil, 50" x 36"*

ONE OF THE MARVELS OF THE WATERY world of bogs, swamps, and woods is the rich bird life. Not only is the Thicket on an important migratory flyway, but it also has enormous rookeries of egrets and herons, which form joint communities in the trees and bushes over places like Village Creek and Turkey Creek.

I had heard of one rookery that was spectacular in its size; tens of thousands of birds called it home. I was making plans to be guided to it, since it was only known to a few people, many of whom were very protective of the site. It was one of the focal points in the on-going controversy over what would and would not be included in the developing park. As the String of Pearls idea was taking shape, meaning the proposed park would claim the chains of creeks and the areas nearest them, there were other locales also screaming for protection.

I was lucky enough to convince a "protective local" to take me to this rookery at sunrise one morning and again at sunset. The apparition of the white birds swirling in the pink and apricot sun was unforgettable. There was a ballet of motion, individual birds leaving one spot only to circle and return to it, but in the meantime another had already taken it over. The returnee settled on the interloper, then both fly up again in a deafening mix of huge wings flapping. I wondered that they did not get seriously hurt or break a wing. But they have been doing this for eons, and the birds seemed to know how to avoid injury. It was comical and gorgeous.

I had learned from my great-grandfather, George B. Dealey, that the *Dallas Morning News* would be dedicated to the idea that every question needed to have both sides presented; something like that is inscribed on the front page of the paper, which he founded. I grew up being taught to keep an open mind. It is apparent to me as a nature lover that unique places deserve protection. However, when families watch government agencies take their land away from them, land they have owned for generations, emotions run high. They do not see it as anything but theft, and the money they may get is little solace for the loss. My grandmother's farm was forcibly taken to create the Dallas–Ft. Worth Airport. Yes, she was paid. Why does anyone think money is as valuable as beloved land? I understand the desperation of older people who often lack the energy to relocate and who feel that losing their land would be practically their own death, knowing the land, their legacy, would not pass on to their children for generations to come.

I heard of the tragedy later. One afternoon, a low-flying duster plane loaded with pesticide flew over the rookery as the innocent birds circled and landed in the trees they called home. The plane made several passes, releasing the poison. By the next day, the entire rookery was wiped out, and the foul stink of their dead, heaped-up bodies lingered for a long time. That is the way some people's minds worked. "If they are going to take my land away from me because of those damn birds, then I'll get rid of them birds and keep my land."

I never knew who was responsible for that act, or for any of various other scenes of destruction that occurred during that war of nature-lovers versus landowners. I have been on both sides of the struggle during my own life. But when I heard about this, I was sick at heart for months.

This painting is my eulogy for those thousands of birds.

PLATE 9. *Pink Rookery at Sunset, 1977, oil, 40" x 50"*

Often the very things

we fear the most

are the things

that get us.

IN THE DARK WATERS THAT FILL THE swamps and streams of the Big Thicket, roots of cypress, water tupelo, and titi reach deep below the surface. The cypress is the master of deep water, sending up knees that bring air to the submerged root system. When I have wandered through a swampy area during a particularly hard drought, the crazy architecture of the exposed root systems looked like life on another planet. The bushes and small trees had sent down countless pillars supporting something like a platform, three to five feet across and resting at the water's usual surface level, from which the tree then resumed its usual growth pattern. With the water gone, the pillars of roots stood free of any vine or grass, looking like a village in New Guinea where the huts are built on posts.

Later, when the rains returned, I sat beside this swamp, musing on the nature of things. Looking deep into the roots of a cypress near me, I saw a huge catfish, feeling too safe there to move at the sight of me. The more I watched, the more I felt I knew something about the look of his underwater world, since I had seen it dry.

But after I painted this, I knew with a jolt that the image was about events going on in my life. At times, there is something I do not want to look at, that I try not to see, that I have disguised so well almost no one sees, at first. That is the "catfish" going on in my life. It is the problem or pain that I deny is there. Yet it looms so large that once it is pointed out you can never fail to see it again.

The little school of fish is an example of the distracting thoughts that I turn to, grateful to see something other than the huge shape of the problem just under the surface.

Despite suffocating emotions, a spiritual approach to life brings the life-giving air to the drowning soul, like the cypress knees. When I face those things I dread and avoid, God gives me the guidance to make my way through them.

PLATE 10. *Catfish Slough, 1978, oil, 48" x 50"*

What is permanent and lasting to us

is merely the transient state

in the long reach of time.

Fretwork of tiny saplings and vines,

lattice of small decisions,

construction of skyscrapers, apartments.

Bondings, joinings of families,

marriages, fights, divorces,

wrenching departures.

All nature is in the same state of flux.

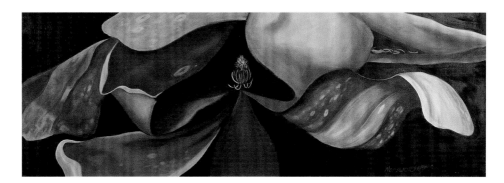

PLATE 11. *Life and Death of the Magnolia* series, *ca. 1980–82, oil*

I HAD A TWENTY-FIVE-FOOT-TALL magnolia in the yard of my studio, just a runt compared to the majestic wonder that had been killed in the Big Thicket. I had a custom of cutting some of the six-inch blooms to bring inside, enjoying their perfume all day.

The day after cutting one bloom, I began to watch it go through the stages of browning, each petal a different shade of buff, ivory, rust, or yellow. The golden stamens fell in a shower and were caught on the petals that remained cupped. I watched for a week as the bloom took on various shapes, the petals curling, browning, and at last falling. During the next few days, the ovary began to grow and swell, pregnant with its seeds.

I had no idea where this was going to take me, but I began to paint the magnolia blooms in all their stages, calling this one the Dowager and another the Matron; there were also the flirty Tart, the young fresh Debutante, and the Nun. In the next few months, the furry seedpods had opened and released their brilliant shiny red seeds, which smelled like turpentine when crushed. The magnolia has an ancient link with conifers from which the turpentine is made. When the seeds fall, the remaining pod has blackened hollows that resemble a snaggle-toothed crone.

I began to paint assemblages, works consisting of three to five paintings, all showing the stages that aging wreaks on the magnolia. Yes, death and rebirth. Never had I imagined that aging could truly be beautiful. I know that in my culture, a man picks a lovely young woman, and when she bears a few children and begins to show signs of wear, he picks a new lovely young woman, just as I used to pick a magnolia bloom and display it in a vase for a day, throwing it away as it began to brown to make room for another freshly picked, snow-white blossom. I was trained to cherish youth.

I thought of the throwaway women in the halfway house I helped found in 1963. We had helped women at Santa Maria Hostel who were disfigured by age, by childbirth, by twisted backs, or by having acid thrown in their faces. I know we all thought these women had no real future because they were no longer young.

In the 1970s, the blast of women's consciousness-raising hit me, and I began to rethink and reexamine all of my values. I painted this series in honor of both the murdered magnolia tree and all the women who feel like throwaways when supplanted by a younger, fresher face. I painted in pain for all the women, including myself, who have believed that clothes, cosmetics, and dieting create their personal value. I needed to see for myself that there is beauty in aging and dignity to be had in dying. This has deeply helped me face the disfigurement of mastectomy and of aging as well as the uncertain nearness of my own death. I have learned to honor my age and to be proud of it. I declare myself a crone, a wise older woman, who has earned her new distinction.

PLATE 12. *Temples and the Parkway, 1981, oil, 24" x 42"*

Daily processions

to the temples of money.

Holy headlights at evening

as the worshippers return,

consumed by

our national religion.

ALL THE TIME I WAS PAINTING THE BIG
Thicket, I had an alter ego of a mother to six children
who went to various schools and had many after-school
activities. Carpooling could only help part of the time.
The afternoons and weekends were spent taking children
to friends, doctors, tutors, and other places. As I drove the
freeways, I began to really notice the columns supporting
the overpasses.

The tunnels and dark shadows of the freeways
intrigued me, and soon I began to see the columns as
tree trunks and the overpasses as the thick upper story of
leaves that shuts out light. But there was also something
very mysterious.

I noticed that our beautiful America, with its jumble
of cultures, lacked one thing that old cultures always
have—namely, a unifying outlook, a set of symbols used
in art, on buildings, and in other aspects of life that have
the same meaning to everyone. The closest we come is
the cross and other Christian images, the Star of David
and some other Jewish symbols, and the popular charac-
ters of Santa Claus and the Easter Bunny.

While I spent hours on the freeway, I thought that

this was surely a unifying act too. The traffic makes you
think the entire city is on the outing right beside you. In
other vehicles you might be passing a family member, a
friend, a business associate, or an adversary. We may not
speak to or even know our neighbors, but at least we
drive next to them every day.

The one ritual the whole city shares is the early-
morning rising and drive to work (or school or elsewhere) and the late-afternoon return. Later, in Bali, I
saw religious processions made almost daily as one or
another holy day was honored. The people got dressed
up in their holiday best and with gongs banging set off
for the river or the temple. How different are their
processions from our traffic? Both cultures believe the
activities to be essential to a good life.

The processions that take place on our freeways are
mostly to honor the one thing that is over-worshipped
in our society: money. We all get up and go to pay
homage to money, to make money, give money, steal
money, and then return home, only to repeat it all the
next day. I noticed that the tallest buildings in the old
towns were the churches, with their spires reaching
heavenward. Today, the tallest buildings are likely to be
corporate office towers owned by banks. There are even
bank buildings in Dallas and Houston that architectur-
ally resemble abstracted churches. Joseph Campbell
spoke of this in interviews with Bill Moyers: Look for
the tallest building, the center of town, or the seat of
power to see the reflected values of the people. Notice
how the most significant buildings have moved over
time from the churches, to the castles, and now to the
office towers.

I wondered what archeologists of a future age might
think when they see all those stone columns, looking
like some Grecian ruin. They might conclude, "Why,
here is where they worshipped!"

PLATE 13. *Can You Get to Heaven on a Flat Tire?*, 1981, oil, 32" x 48"

Long Draw

Hot summer middays, riding

a horse that crushes under foot

herbs, roots, flowers, lemoncilla, fragrances

that live with me forever.

A quick rain

cools us,

wakens the creosote bush

suffusing the desert

with its clean herbal scent.

Chapter 2

CALL OF THE DESERT

BIG BEND IS DESERT, AT ONCE HOT, rocky, and thorny. It seems indifferent to the visitor. There is no apparent welcome, no shelter, and no safety.

I had been told by three people, "Jeanne, your niche is in the Big Bend."

It sounded like they were saying "Big Ben," referring to the clock in London. What is Big Bend? At last someone explained that it was where the Rio Grande (the river that flows upstream, someone called it) makes a huge elbow turn north and creates a bulge in the southern border of Texas. Others told me the region was desert and mountains. Why should *that* seem to be my niche to other people? I was living in warm, muggy, lush, subtropical Houston, where the azaleas swell up and fill the city with blooms each spring and where low, scudding gulf clouds pass close to the tops of pines and water oaks. How do these folks see me, I wondered. I lived in River Oaks, in a mansion, surrounded with luxury, and yet there are people who see through that and tell me I belong in a desert. Thank God they can see through that!

When I first arrived in Big Bend, it put on the show of the century. I drove the twelve hours out there

Blair Pittman

with Blair Pittman, my soon-to-be husband. He owned land in the Big Bend and raved about the desert and mountains.

As we began the descent out of mile-high Alpine, the clouds began to hold colorful sundogs, small captured rainbows of rose, gold, and green; sometimes, as we rounded a turn, there was a full rainbow. Ahead of us, dark sheets of rain were falling in the distance. The afternoon light was deepening, and the landscape

changed from the rolling high hills of Alpine to something Blair called the Flats. In all directions I saw flat desert with jagged mountains in the distance, pale blue against the sky. The shadows of passing clouds turned some mountains nearly black. It was a mosaic of light play.

Blair was thrilled to be heading for the mountains. I am a flatlander, a true flatlander. On the prairies of Dallas I had learned to love the sky! Mountains had so far only faintly interested me. Yet here was sky enough for hundreds of paintings. We were both visual artists, so as I grew enthusiastic about the lighting in the sky, he paused to agree, but got increasingly excited about the idea of the nearing mountains.

We stopped at a road cut that became to me the symbolic Gates to Big Bend. As I looked through the narrow opening, the whole landscape tilted precariously down toward the Rio Grande, pulled by the Terlingua fault. Mountaintops spread out in layers before me, and the light and shadow ran quickly over the ridges, changing shapes dramatically. I always stop there now on a return trip, both to let my dogs out and to let the heart of the Big Bend fill me.

Blair and I were hurriedly back in the jeep, and we dipped down the steep hill as he put the Jeep in neutral and coasted at fifty miles an hour, taking us down into a valley enclosed by severe ridges of rock. Waving his hand, he said, "There is Luna Vista."

I glanced to the right and saw a deserted-looking stone building with a porch. It used to be a home and a restaurant. I reflected on the last one hundred miles of nothing (to my big-city eyes): Absolutely no signs of human habitation. I had seen shambles of stores, attempts at houses, and gates with dirt roads leading off, I thought, to nowhere.

As we flew down the narrow two-lane highway,

Blair pointed to an arroyo, and I saw a dry creek bed with a narrow stream of water as we drove across it. In later years this became a spot well known to me as a sure place to be caught by floodwaters. I have spent many hours at that crossing, waiting for the water to recede. There lived nearby an eccentric man named Emil, said to be a nuclear physicist, who escaped to the Big Bend in order to drink in peace. He kept several cases of beer in his back seat, and I often saw him at the bridge drinking happily, waiting for that arroyo to go down.

Starting up the other side, there is a very steep ascent, hell if you are pulling a trailer. The old Jeep pointed its nose to the sky and slowed; on this trip we had watched the odometer roll over to read 100,000 miles. Blair shifted into first gear and we roared slowly up a winding, turning path through peculiar cliffs of red, brown, and black rocks. Actually, this was the mountains, I realized, and sadly noted that I was not excited but rather irritated that I could not see out as easily, an admission that I did not understand how to view this place. What is so wonderful about a lot of angular red-brown rock? I was greatly relieved that the Jeep succeeded in making it this far, though.

As we crested I saw before me the most peculiar jumble of clay hills, yellow and gray, and sudden unexplained ridges of rocks running like fencerows spread out before me. Mountains of all sorts crowded together. Some had soft, folded rocky sides, looking much like poured chocolate fudge before it sets. Another had straight thin columns of rock around a central area of curved thin columns. My inner artist was becoming unsettled. What could you do with this landscape, all this rock? How do you paint rocks and not have them look like marshmallows? I soon learned that painting a rock is as intricate as a portrait of a person.

Above us was an enormous double rainbow hanging in radiance, and I knew that a place that had this kind of glory would somehow contain other glories I would come to know.

Meanwhile, I tapped my scattered knowledge of geology. We passed a strange pile of regular, square black rocks atop a clay hill.

"I think those are volcanic," I said, not knowing the whole area was stirred and tossed by volcanism.

"No," said Blair, "that's just rock. There is mostly limestone out here." Limestone was his true love.

"Gotta be volcanic."

"No."

"Hmmm . . . can't even use my geology out here."

Thunderheads swirl, advance, grow, blow,

flashing with multitudes of lights.

The raging hailstorms or the sweet blessing of

    rain

move across the desert with the

deliberate smoothness of Queen Elizabeth,

commanding respect as she billowed with layers

of skirts, puffy sleeves, volumes of satin and

    velvet.

The flash in her eye, like the flash of her

    jewels,

delivered menace or blessing.

THE RAINBOW ROSE HIGHER NOW AS the sun turned orange and prepared to set. We arrived at Villa de la Mina, tore out the cameras, and raced to a high hill to see the rain pouring in a golden curtain through the sunlight and the navy clouds dusted with orange. A powerful wind was blowing, and I had to lean to stand upright.

"That rain is falling in Terlingua," Blair hollered against the wind, "the Ghost Town."

To the west the sun was dramatically lighting crisp edges of rock and yucca. To the southwest rain was slanting into the sunlight, and to the south a large gust of wind was pushing a wall of dust that glowed golden. To the east the rainbow was intensifying. I learned what Blair meant when he talked about "Big Bend doing its magic." It was as if Jennifer Tifton, the wonderful stage-lighting expert, had been given the command to light the stage. The rainbow became the first and only red bow I have ever seen. It glowed an unbelievable red, and a beam of golden light shone out from its center across the desert. The limestone mountains of Reed Plateau were dazzling gold with a backdrop of red, and on the opposite side of the sky to the west, the sunset was also "carrying on." In between the two "stage sets," the clouds were dark navy. I got at least two paintings out of that moment and enough assurance that I should hold off any snap judgments about this locale that was supposed to be my "niche." Patience has never been an easy virtue for me.

PLATE 14. *Storm over Terlingua, 1985, oil, 34" x 44"*

There is a way that science

enhances mystery,

even as it explains it.

BIG BEND WELCOMED ME ON MY FIRST trip with one spectacular display after another, one of which was the red bow, a weather anomaly. I did not know what to think about it then, and I still do not know today what to think about the things that followed. But they so determined my path that I cannot leave them out.

Twenty years ago I was invited to accompany a friend to a spaghetti party given by a girl named Marcia Sleeper. Or was it Diane, or Margaret? It was the last name that froze in my brain. I knew I had to meet her. There was something that was going to be important about my knowing her. When I met her, though, there was nothing, flat nothing, and I could not believe it. The unsought "knowings" are always significant, so I asked her if she had sisters or brothers. A brother, she told me, in high school. That is not it, I decided, and tried to forget it all.

Years later on this drive to Big Bend, Blair reviewed the names of people in the local community, and I heard him mention David Sleeper. I was absently looking at a certain mesa to one side of Interstate 10, which became branded onto my brain, the formation glowing somehow with the name Sleeper. Blair continued talking, but I was in a somewhat numb and blank daze, just the name, Sleeper. A certainty filled me. There was that peculiar name again, this time with my even more peculiar

reaction added. I heard nothing else about him, but there was that name again, and this time I was sure I was going to meet the Sleeper that I had felt such energy about twenty years earlier.

One night while camping on the Land, as Blair affectionately called his forty acres, he prepared to grill steaks over mesquite. I cautiously decided to check out the effect of the name Sleeper, so sipping my Dr. Pepper I casually asked for another review of the folks in the area. Pouring an Usher's scotch, Blair began to ramble on about everyone. When he unexpectedly said that name again, said folks just called him "Sleeper," inwardly I felt the hills around me roll in waves to a deep earth drumbeat. I was in a trance. "Where," I managed to ask, "does he live?"

"About up that way," Blair pointed toward Long Draw, "in a ghost town called Buenos Suerte."

Another ghost town. I looked up Long Draw, missing the rest of Blair's description. Silently I asked, "God, or my Inner Guidance, or please someone . . . what does this mean?" There came an answer, certain, as if from outside of me.

"Your guru . . . Your lover . . . Your friend." (As if I could chose any one of the three.)

Then one last message, "For life."

Stunned, I asked, inwardly, "What about him?" glancing at Blair, who was turning the steaks over a spicy mesquite-wood fire.

There was no answer, but I saw someone shrug and I understood. It made no difference what I did or did not do with Blair. This Sleeper was in the wings preparing to make an entrance, and fate would see to it . . . whenever. I understood that he could be either friend, lover, guru, or all three, but it would be for life. I thought this Sleeper might be a wise old man, someone I could learn from.

PLATE 15. *Red Bow over Reed Plateau, 1985, oil, 14" x 22"*

I envisioned Blair and me having great talks with this old man, since Blair seemed to have admiration for him.

I married Blair and we went to Big Bend many times a year. The fourth year of our marriage was a rough one for me. We knew it was over, but we held together until the end of that year, because my daughter was getting married. We divorced shortly afterward.

I did not seek out that Sleeper man. Although I was curious, I was not eager to see him. This was a certainty within me, and it was important that I wait for something that rushing would spoil. Whatever would happen with Sleeper would unfurl, uncoil, and reveal itself when the time was ready.

Blair and I continued to travel to the Big Bend, hoping each time we could mend our fraying marriage. On our last trip, we walked into a noisy dance at Lajitas, and Blair said, "There's David Sleeper."

I heard inside, "It's begun."

PLATE 16.
Clay Hills
with Indian
Banding,
1984, oil,
28" x 35"

Seems to me

all great artists

must surely have

deep, mystical convictions.

Lukewarm attitudes

kill creativity.

To create is to take a stand.

You must know what

question to ask in order

to find the answer

in the work of art.

GEOLOGY QUESTIONS PUZZLE EVERYONE who visits Big Bend. Throughout the area are clay hills with multicolored bands of maroon, red, pink, peach, orange, yellow, cream, buff, tan, and white. Especially strange are the areas where the white takes on an aqua tint and the rocks are all shades of green, from kelly to olive. I was certain it was a sign of copper in some form, maybe malachite waiting to be discovered in some hills. I checked the volcanic rocks for olivine but found none. However, I was sure that the varying shades of yellow found in a certain road cut were some form of sulfur, or maybe zinc. Who knows?

ARCH, Badlands, Lajitas

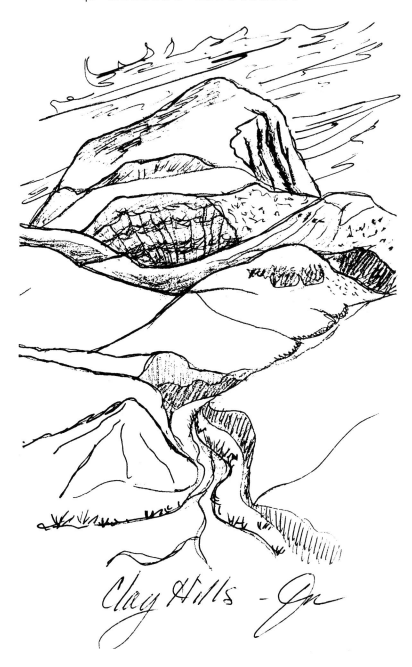

Clay Hills — Jn

My question was, "How do I paint these multicolored clay hills and how do I turn them into a work of art?" I decided that composition was their essence and beauty the justification. I understood my challenge even better when I spent a day curled up at the feet of Big Bend's geology expert, Dr. Ross Maxwell, who was leading a three-day tour I attended.

"What are the minerals that create those multitudes of colors?" I asked, adding that artists need to be very aware of minerals and their interactions in paint colors.

"Chlorite," came his terse answer.

Chlorite? We passed a road cut of yellow and to my question came the reply again, "Chlorite."

We passed the aquatinted area, and I was sure this time that there would be some interesting mineral action to hear about. He said again, briefly, "That's just chlorite. I've tested all these places myself years ago, and chlorite makes all these colors."

I protested. "But doesn't some other mineral interact to make the changes, like manganese or something? These are like the colors in my tubes of paint, which are made from hundreds of different minerals."

"No," he turned to look at me, smiling at my persistence, "nothing interesting. Iron in the chlorite makes all the colors you see."

Later, when we talked about some hawks flying above, he commented that he only knew of two kinds of birds: sparrows and ducks. If the birds are little, they are sparrows, if they are big, ducks. Dissatisfied with the answers to my questions on minerals, I wondered if he thought colors were either chlorite or not chlorite!

THE VIEW INTO MEXICO IS BLOCKED from Fresno Ranch by a three-hundred-foot cliff rising from the river that I call the Great Wall of Chihuahua. It is impassable except for a canyon that runs through the center of Rancho Picachos, which I bought in 1985. The pass branches out into a maze of wide and narrow canyons in the Picachos Mountains, which means in Spanish "especially jagged, pointy peaks."

Many things have happened on Rancho Picachos that were special because it often had different rainfall than we had in Texas just across the river, fifty feet away. All the beauty that was quietly happening behind the Great Wall of Chihuahua was occurring unseen and unsung until we broke into the midst of it all.

There is no way to travel over that land but on foot or on horseback; I will never hike if I can ride. The vastness of the desert cannot be traversed safely on foot, especially if you want your water supply to last the trip. So I would always make the long trips on my Paso Fino, Altivo, with saddlebags loaded with bean and jalapeno burritos, apples, an army surplus water bladder, art supplies, spare jacket, cameras, and binoculars.

The trail starts by climbing through three thousand acres of volcanic mountains that reach higher and higher until they crest, and then over the top and down you go, descending precariously over limestone and dagger-like lechuguilla that curves upward, ready to stab your horse repeatedly with stinging needles. The back two thousand acres are filled with clusters of plants that prefer to live in limestone rather than volcanic rock, more candelilla, less Indian paintbrush, and more lavender asters.

Turning east and traveling about a mile, we come to an abandoned mine. The miners set themselves up to produce mercury, and every time they fired up the retort, it blew up. At last an assayer from Cuidad Chihuahua

arrived and determined that the explosions were caused by the presence of uranium. So they rebuilt the system and produced uranium for a few years. Using the white limestone, they built a regular little village, which is now a crumbled ghost town, resembling the old Terlingua (before it was recently "discovered" and revitalized). I was especially grateful that the market had fallen out for uranium, since there is plenty of that ore on the Texas side too. We could have been living in the middle of the very pollutants we left the cities to escape.

In Mexico the landowner never owns the minerals and is powerless if the government decides it wants to come in and dig. So I would have had no way to stop the mine from being active again, if there had been money in it for Mexico.

Nature herself was not doing such a good job of keeping pollutants out either. One day I saw a young woman named Jennifer, who worked for some government branch, testing the river water at the weir near Presidio. I was there letting my dog, Bruja, have a run before we began the fifty-mile trip back home. Jennifer said that at the mouth of each canyon and arroyo there are so many dissolved heavy metals such as uranium, arsenic, selenium, and mercury that she wanted to wash her hands after touching the water. Those minerals wash in from the exposed slopes of the canyons and mountains from both Texas and Mexico. I stared in new horror as my beloved dog rushed into the river to cool off and drink. All our animals swam in and drank from the river daily. We lived along it. However, we never ate the fish from that river, for even before Jennifer's warning we knew of the sewage and poisons coming in from the Rio Conchos in Mexico, the farmlands on both sides of the border, and the American towns all the way back up to my fellow river-neighbors in New Mexico.

PLATE 17. *Abandoned Uranium Mine, 1987, oil, 42" x 36"*

When I painted this mine, I remembered the huge cumulus thunderstorms that piled up in summer, teasing us with promise of rain. I put in a storm, the anvil-headed kind, because it reminds me of the mushroom cloud that forms from the explosion of an atom bomb. I thought of the toxins that contaminate our great river. My prayer is that nuclear warfare will somehow be abandoned like this mine and that we will somehow stop poisoning our precious waters. I think about this abandoned mine with joy that its deadly product is no longer in great demand.

We must heal our home, our earth, before we ourselves can be safe and whole.

Wonder how people learned

to set up rocks

that tell the seasons?

Nature provided them

with her own Stonehenges.

Wise men and women observed,

then began to imitate Her.

SOME MORNINGS IN THE DESERT, I WOULD wake to see in the west just one mountain glowing with a golden color. There was no clear explanation of the effect nor of why it would have a narrow focus and cover just one peak. I might witness this only once or twice a year. After many years of thinking about all the other strange lighting effects that I had seen, I decided I might have the answer to this particular one. I think there is a chink between two mountains through which the morning sun can peek, perhaps at only two times during the year. The rest of the time the sun has risen so high before its direct rays hit the mountains to the west that it has lost its morning apricot color.

I came to this conclusion partly from trying to see the rising full moon at its most orange, realizing that the mountains blocked my view except at certain spots. There is that glorious rising and setting of sun and moon one sees on the beach at a place like Galveston that is lost when you are surrounded by high mountains. But by compensation, the way the sun paints the mountains cannot be done to anything on the flatlands, where nothing sticks up over skyscraper height. It is those mountains, rising up an extra five hundred or a thousand feet, that catch the very first incredible golden rays, so dense in color even the brown rocks turn yellow and gold. It is even more rare because if the sun is lined up right on, say, March 12 and September 12, but a bank of clouds appears in the east that morning, you will not see it. You could miss the effect several years in a row. But when the backdrop is a sky full of indigo storm clouds, and the "Stage Manager" then turns that gold spotlight on my favorite Poster Peak, I know I am in for a show.

PLATE 18. *Morning Sun on Poster Peak, 1996, oil, 47" x 48"*

The sacred places of early people

are empowered

by the reverence and prayers

of generations.

When you feel it,

you are special too.

IN THIS UNIQUE CANYON, PAINTED symbols on the rocky walls serve as reminders of the early Indians who lived here. These offer a sense of their lives and their prayers, of the women who ground the many *metate* holes. This was a sacred place to the early people. Underneath a certain rock ledge is the entire skeleton of a fish fossilized in the rock. Don't you wonder what marvelous story that must have provoked among those people?

As nature guarded and protected the sanctity of the canyon, gargoyles were carved into the walls by wind and water. These beings watch possessively when humans arrive, attempting to feel comfortable and at home in the gargoyles' protectorate.

For those who do not maintain respect for the past, for the rocks and walls, the pictographs, the water, and the integrity of the silence, an uneasy discomfort sets in. The watchful Beings unfold their powers. A rock falls, crashing nearby. A startled person slips into a *tinaja* (a large or small hole in limestone filled with black water), then struggles to get a handhold to climb out. Raucous laughter is heard, is it a raven? Faces seem to appear on the canyon walls. Fear sets in.

For those who "belong," however, the Beings whisper to one another approvingly of the visitor. A dark cave beckons. An owl silently arrives to guard the visitor, amphibious creatures timidly rise up from the depths of a bottomless *tinaja* to watch the welcomed one, and the stone speaks of time, of truth, of spirits, and of things hidden.

PLATE 19. *Canyon de las Brujas, 1986, oil, 50" x 38"*

PLATE 20. *Rain at Rancho Saus, 1987, oil, 40" x 50"*

THE ARTIST LYNN RANDOLPH, A FRIEND who also paints many pictures in a Big Bend setting, came out to visit me. She was excited and wanted to see all the magic places, but Lynn was not at all thrilled that she would have to travel by horseback. However, her need to see overcame her need to be safe. In fact, I gave her my personal horse to ride, promising her that he was the most trustworthy animal.

I also reluctantly agreed not to travel faster than a walk. Many seasoned riders, like myself, who no longer get sore from horseback riding, do get quite uncomfortable after a long day merely walking. If beginners complain about getting sore when riding, it is probably because they travel at a walk. The slower pace meant refiguring the whole day's schedule, because at a walk we would not go very far. It was drizzling, a happy novelty in the desert, but probably a bore to a Houstonite who deals with drizzle frequently. Nonetheless, off we went, crossing the Rio Grande to my ranch in Mexico. Lynn was a good sport.

We slowly wound up a trail that led to the cliff overlooking the river and Fresno Ranch. I was completely unprepared for what happened next. The clouds broke to the west and the late-afternoon sun turned the desert into a stage setting. Over our heads hung a huge double rainbow cast on a nearby rain shower, very brilliant and appearing nearby. Inside the center bow, after the usual color display, there were repeating bows of magenta and green. I have never seen that before or since.

To the east the magnificent Chisos Mountains floated in a shifting pattern of golden sun one minute and dark navy shadow the next. To the north the mysterious Solitario was still caught in a passing shower. All around us in Mexico, the volcanic mountains were coated with a green blanket that looked so soft from a distance, which is misleading, because nothing is soft in Big Bend. Probably a lot of the green was ocotillo, resurrection fern, mesquite, and the creosote bush restored to a deep green resembling conifers. At our feet were thousands of clumps of asters, little yellow flowers that some naturalists call "DLYs" (damnlittleyellows) that I could not identify, and the wonderful rosettes of thousands of resurrection ferns, which open when it rains. The rosettes roll back up like a porch shade when they dry out, barely showing up then, brown against brown rock. But when open, they are a deep, rich glowing green.

Now the Solitario was free of clouds, and the slick wet flatirons that adorn that nine-mile circle were white in the sun, shining like snow. To the east my Mexican neighbor's ranch was receiving a shower, which was lit up by the sun; this is what I painted in *Rain at Rancho Saus*. The ride that day inspired many more paintings such as *Shaman Summoning My Broken Spirit*.

The most wonderful lesson to me from that day was Lynn's courage to persevere—on a horse, in the rain, crossing the Rio Grande, and trusting it would be worth it. While I myself, suspecting all the way the ride was going to be dreary, found out that many treasures are earned through trust and risk.

How many times

do I have to learn

that even doing things grudgingly

can turn out to have

unexpected rewards?

THERE WAS ONLY ONE AUTUMN DURING which a combination of rain and cool evenings produced hillsides of living jewel boxes. Usually the leaves of leatherstem, if there are any at all, are simply yellow or brown in the fall. The leatherstem, frequently barren of leaf like the ocotillo and many other desert plants, fleshed itself out this year just in time to turn with autumn colors. I would never have known about this if not for the need to play hostess one day.

Folks had arrived and expected to be shown a good horseback ride. We rode our mounts upstream along the Rio Grande to the hard-bottomed ford that is always the shallowest place to cross. Because of recent rains, though, the water was high enough that day to force us to take our feet out of the stirrups, cross them over the pommel, and rest them on the horses' shoulders, otherwise we would have very wet boots. This was usually exciting for a visitor. I suspected this might be the greatest thrill they got out of the ride, for they were not the "looking" kind of company but rather real chatterboxes who seemed to only want high adventure, like perhaps a run at break-

neck speed through obviously dangerous terrain. We did not get visitors of that sort very often, and I was not looking forward to being begged to run the horses. That is why I thought a ride through the deep volcanic rocks in the front half of Rancho Picachos might help me handle them better.

We entered the first canyon, which was cool and shady, and then as we rounded a bend, the late afternoon sun bore down upon us. All at once the leatherstem that filled the slopes of the mountains lit up like Christmas trees, their translucent leaves shining with the sun behind them. Each small bush had its own color of gold, yellow, apricot, peach, pink, magenta, red, or blends of all. The color had not been noticeable out in the desert flats or atop the mesas, since the leaves needed the cool canyon nights to do the trick. This was not apparent walking through the shade either, where there were no special lighting effects.

Once again, the canyons and mountains behind the Great Wall were having their own private fiesta. I have seen only one photograph of this in the public domain, and it was taken by Lawrence Parent, who has a wonderful eye and has captured many things that very few people see. I have often wondered if he found his display in Big Bend National Park, which is at a higher elevation where there is a greater chance for cool evenings and rain to help create such a beautiful sight.

On the way back home, the guests were still talking, hollering to each other over the clatter of horseshoes on rocks. In the midst of ocotillo blooming brilliant red from the out-of-season rain, I found the only ocotillo with yellow blooms I had ever seen.

Back at the tack room, unsaddling the horses as my guests said how they loved the ride, I mused how they

PLATE 21. *Backlit Leatherstem, 1987, oil, 20" x 30"*

probably had not appreciated that leatherstem, no doubt because they thought that it happens every year. Since the desert is rather foreign to most city people, every

magical thing is accepted as an everyday event. It took me several years to recognize the unusual, the once-in-a-lifetime sight or event. This day had given me one more.

PLATE 22. *Carlotta Tinaja, 1987, oil, 40" x 50"*

All doors

can be entered

by either side.

THIS MAGICAL PLACE WAS SHOWN TO ME
by a friend who told me to sleep there and see the
surprise in the water in the morning light. Her name was
Donna, but we all knew her as the Bat Lady; she had two
pet fruit bats that flew around her bedroom at night.
Donna was a biologist working for the government. I
took her advice and visited the place with my bedroll
and my dog, Bruja. It seemed impossible that anyone
could find this *tinaja* unless one either fell off the road
into it by mistake or knew someone who could serve as
guide. It is so hidden, and all the landscape nearby is so
flat, that one would never suspect there was something
this beautiful right beside the road.

   In the early morning, Donna was up making a bat
count and waiting for me to wake up. She said softly,

"Look into the water, and tell me where that tunnel's
reflection comes from." I looked from my bedroll. I then
stood up. I walked around. The tunnel seemed to have no
counterpart in the real rock wall. At last I figured it out,
but not before I was transported back to stories I had
read as a child. So much of what we think is real is only
an illusion, and those illusions can seem to be more solid
than reality.

   This painting is also a metaphor for entering
another world. I like to imagine diving into that opening and emerging into another realm, like in children's
stories such as *The Lion, the Witch, and the Wardrobe* or
Raggedy Ann and Andy (in which the two dolls found a
magic tree with a trapdoor inside, opening up to another world).

   What I love about this is that there is a scientific
reason for the reflection, but it was very hard at first for
me to understand it. I had to walk around the pool,
looking from different angles, until I "saw" the reality.
When objective truth and magic merge, people see the
wonder of the world as does a child, or perhaps a shaman. And it is in these times, I have learned, that real
healing can occur in ways science cannot explain, even
though the undeniable fact is there, mystifying doctors
and scientists.

Owls + others
JN

Chapter 3

SIREN NIGHT SONG

Big Bend is a land where

mountains reach

to touch the sky,

ever out of reach.

Big Bend goes up and up

through the clouds,

past the stars,

and beyond.

I MARRIED DAVID SLEEPER EIGHTEEN months after meeting him. My house went on the market in Houston, and though I expected that the sale would take two years, it sold in four days. My two youngest children wanted to live with their dad, and they were legally old enough to make that decision. I was stunned. It was like the Red Sea parting for Moses: there were no obstacles left. It was 1982 and time to move to Fresno.

When I first moved to Fresno Ranch it was more like camping out. As you read how I lived, remember, I was having a ball! There were two other people on the ranch—David, with his long blond beard and hair, and his younger brother, Mark, with a short black beard and dark hair. The challenges were fun, and David and Mark were full of jokes and pranks.

The ranch had been abandoned for forty years and looked like it. The Sleeper brothers were poor, "patching patches with patches." Rex Ivey Sr., who had owned most of Terlingua and Lajitas at one time or another, had moved the main adobe house piece by piece from Terlingua to Fresno thirty years before, so it had that golden color of Terlingua clay. There had once been a bathroom floored with unusual tiles with patterns pressed into them, which are no longer found in Ojinaga, Mexico. Whatever fixtures and pipes had been there originally no longer worked and had been pulled out; all that remained was a drain for the nonexistent shower. Now the bathroom was a pantry, lined with shelves. There was no door. An old blanket hung in the doorway in winter to spare us heating that small room.

The washtubs were large garbage cans, one for soaking horse-stained jeans in soapy water and another for rinsing. We used a broomstick to stir the mess. The fence, made of small-gauge train track from the mines in Terlingua, doubled as a clothesline. Never did that rail fence put a stain on the wet clothes, it was sealed with "desert varnish."

The west wall of the house was badly cracked, and the wind blew through, fluttering the flame in my kerosene lantern as I ate and read at night. We had no electricity.

Western Side of Solitario + Headwaters for
Fresno Creek —Jn

Water was run by gravity from Fresno Creek in pipes laid straight to the house. No one lived anywhere upstream, and we drank that water not only in the house but also anytime we were out riding by the creek. Its headwaters were miles away, originating in the Solitario, and bolstered in its course by many springs.

When it rained, if it rained, we described it as either a three-bucket or a full ten-bucket rain. That meant that a brief shower required no more than three buckets in the house to catch the leaks from the roof, but a long, hard rain typically fed leaks in ten places. The annual rainfall is only eight inches, so this was not a frequent concern. The floor was smooth gray concrete and could not be damaged. I learned, however, that the cracks in the floor might go as deep as China.

Ant attacks were a daily occurrence. I learned to kill the pests with dish soap on a wet paper towel and then spray their entrance, which could be under the sink, in a wall, or from the depths below the floor. I learned to track their trails on my hands and knees with a flashlight. Then I would fill up that entrance with transparent silicon gel. Slowly over the years, the ant attacks lessened. After about five years, I decided to try to fill the cement cracks in the floor, which also allowed ants into the room. After pulling out the loose pieces, I saw that I could push in fresh cement, then more, and even more, until I gave up. It looked like there was a massive cavity under the house.

One day, Mark came over from the renovated goat shed he had converted into his home and said, "From the looks of what I see in the back yard, you must have heard a pretty loud noise last night." We went out to see, and there was a wide crack running along the ground that went directly under the house and disappeared. We had heard that geologists from Southern Methodist University in Dallas had set up seismographs all around the Big Bend, reporting up to a hundred small quakes a day. It is believed that this constant movement prevents energy from building up into large earthquakes. This new crack was one of many small signs of the constantly moving earth and explained why some houses cracked up so easily.

Our wood-burning stove was ancient, from Iowa, and had a childproof lining around it, thus barely putting out any heat. In winter if we worked at it, we could get the stove to raise the temperature to about forty degrees at three feet from the drafty floor. The room got warmer as you moved toward the ceiling until, at the top, it would be seventy degrees. I wore every kind of long johns I could find, two shirts, and a sweater, usually eating dinner with a blanket over my lap. I bought winter shoes one size too big and wore two pairs of thick socks.

We slept outside on a screened porch. The tiny house had only a kitchen and living room. During winter I kept a pillow over my head, since sleeping caps slipped off. I had to learn from my Yankee husband that covering the head is one of the most important ways to stay warm. Until we got a down comforter, David and I put so many blankets over us that I could hardly turn over for the weight of them.

THIS SNAKE, THE WESTERN COACHWHIP, is only found red in Big Bend; elsewhere it is tan or yellow-ocher. It has a right to live in the desert as much as I do or anyone else. I learned not to desecrate the desert after seeing tourists collecting items day and night. At night I could hear them on the highway, starting and stopping, car doors opening and closing, digging and collecting cactus, snakes, and rocks, all under the protection of dark night.

I saw scorpions. One was often on the screen door, eating bugs attracted by the light at dinnertime. I used that door to go in or out, but a scorpion never stung me. I was pretty careless after a while. I never tried to kill the scorpions, for I was glad they were on bug duty. I hoped they would eat the blasted *chupa sangre,* kissing bugs, or conenose bugs, crafty, sneaky, and determined pests that are black with red markings and usually arrived in May. They would fly into the room at night, crash into a wall, and hit the floor. As soon as I heard that crash, sounding like a June bug colliding with an object, I would be up, looking. The *chupa sangre* are attracted to women more than men, sneaking up as you sleep to suck your blood. I suspect the female beetles are prowling for the hormones in the woman to trigger their own fertility cycle, because wherever a man and woman sleep together, the woman always receives the most bites. The bite itches wildly for weeks and turns large, angry red, and disfiguring if located on the face and neck. Nothing relieves this reaction except not scratching, which took me several years to learn.

The toilet at Fresno Ranch was a hole in the ground dug with a shovel. We each chose our favorite out-of-the-way spot, dug the hole, and after using it covered it up with the dirt from the hole we dug beside it for our next visit. In time this made a long covered-up trench, and when we reached a spot too far away to walk, we just turned the trenching back parallel to the first. The rule was: "Make the hole deep enough so that you wouldn't mind putting your bedroll over it."

Another rule was no toilet paper. It did not biodegrade fast enough, and the dogs liked to dig it up. If anyone had to use it, it had to be burned afterward. Try burning wet toilet paper. Try even getting the match to stay lit on a windy day. The alternative to paper was a smooth rock. I quickly saw the advantages of this and kept a pile of smooth rocks chosen from the creek near my trench. As each was buried away, I collected more. I had water in a wonderful plastic shampoo squeeze-bottle with a fold-down spout. I took it with me, and together with a rock, I had a system as good as any bidet. I felt cleaner than in the city. The cool water felt great in the desert heat. And who could not love squatting, in nature's preferred position, while red-tailed hawks circle and cry and a covey of scaled quail run past? Far more interesting than reading a magazine in the bathroom!

Soon all of our house animals began to follow me down the path I took to the creek vega, where there was a deep sand cover. The two cats dug their holes, the three to four dogs wandered off and did their business, and I would laugh at the sense of community they all provided me.

PLATE 23. *This Land Is My Land, 1987, oil, 43" x 28"*

THERE ARE MANY SYMBOLS FOR ancient religions, most of which are nearly forgotten. The Owl was the escort for the goddess in many parts of the Old World, for instance, Athena. The Owl is still feared by Mexican men of the border, as they believe it foretells misfortune. That is one of many old ways sacred to goddess religions that have been perverted from their original meanings. The full moon has been blamed for disasters, for lunatics, and for all types of insanities, but women once revered it. It is intimately associated with women still. After a year had passed from completion of this painting, someone pointed out to my amazement that the clouds resemble fallopian tubes. I guess they do.

I used a gold underpaint for the sky and then glazed the purple over it to produce the unique glow that hangs in the desert sky long after twilight. The skyline is of Mule Ears, a formation in Big Bend National Park. David Sleeper and I got permission to ride there one day, and I have never seen a more mysterious place anywhere than that small mountain. It was really spooky, which is saying a lot, for there are many strange places in the Big Bend—and I thought I was used to unusual sights.

The mountain known as Mule Ears is like the Horned One, associated with most goddesses of the grain. The horns of the cow used to plow also lent the half-moon shape associated with goddess images found in Europe and in Mexico. Look at the image of Our Lady of Guadalupe. You may believe she stands on the sickle moon, like Mary in the Miraculous Medal. But look again. If you are examining a faithful reproduction, the sickle is gray with black ends. Horns! How ironic. Something once sacred to the goddess religions was overlooked by the church and is promulgated all across Mexico.

Early Christianity, still fighting against the goddesses, needed to redefine forever those things holy to the goddess and instill them with new evil connotations. It chose to create a devil and gave him horns and cloven feet, parts of one of the holiest symbols, the simple cow. Many Indians used buffalo-horn headdresses in their sacred rituals, for that animal was also a life giver and revered. I wonder how Native Americans today feel, knowing the Nazis appropriated the sacred symbol of the Four Directions (what became the swastika), a deeply spiritual and mysterious part of Native American religions. When I first saw swastikas on old Indian blankets I was horrified. I knew so little then of how certain symbols get used over and over through the ages and how their meaning sometimes changed to the exact opposite of the original connotation.

It bothers me how women also became rejected in religion, displaced, and not allowed to act as spiritual leaders or healers. I was once a devout Catholic (but now am a recovering Catholic). This painting is also a reminder of all that was once Mother God's power and her holy objects. Although much has been reviled, or usurped, by the patriarchy, I personally take comfort in knowing there was a time when things female were considered sacred.

The flowers are known in many ways. To ranchers, they are the deadly Jimson weed, dreaded and hated for the deaths it causes when eaten by livestock. To me, they are beautiful, fragrant wonders that bloom only at night, closing in the midmorning. To early people, they were known as the Sacred Datura. The holy women, the healer-women, knew how to distill the plant and use it to produce a trancelike state for prophesying. They also knew how to use it to ease the pangs of childbirth.

Women's Ancient Mysteries was painted with all these things in mind.

PLATE 24. *Women's Ancient Mysteries, 1989, oil, 44" x 48"*

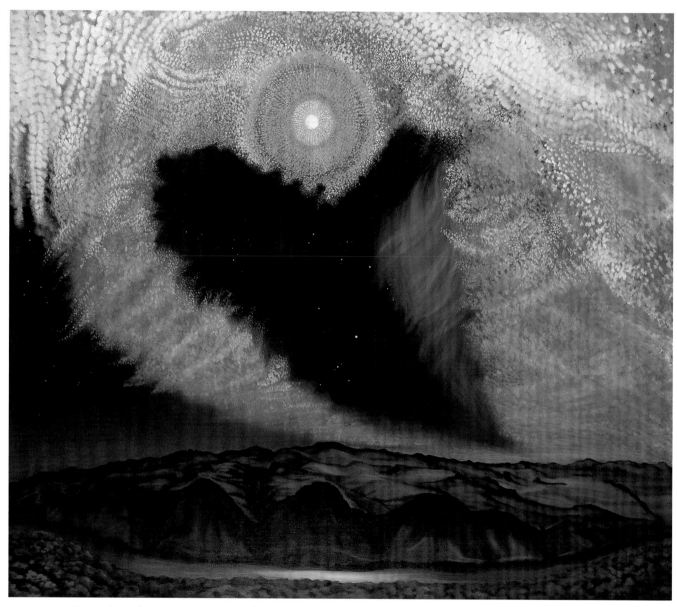

PLATE 25. *Love Song from Mexico, 1990, oil, 48" x 56"*

ONE DAY MY HUSBAND TOOK THE bulldozer across the low water of the Rio Grande to dig a new water tank for the longhorn cattle on my ranch in Mexico. He stayed in a cave for three nights until the work was finished. I moved into my studio, painting somewhat 'round the clock, uninterrupted by any need to cook or do most other household chores. I love to paint for long, uninterrupted hours, which can be hard on the people in my life.

Late one evening, I went outside to take a break and saw this sky. I ran back inside for pencils and paper and then raced back out to draw, by the light of the moon, all the details of the cloud patterns. Right away I stretched a new canvas and began this painting.

When my husband came home, the piece was finished. He took one look and exclaimed, "Well, you got my message!" Since we had no phone and no runner had come bearing news, I was confused. He explained that two nights before he had seen this same sky before

going to sleep and had focused hard on sending me the message to go outside, saying, "Jeanne, go and look! It's your favorite clouds!"

Maybe I did get that message, for I had abruptly dropped my paintbrush that night and walked outside without thinking. After I returned outside with my paper and pencil, I stood transfixed, sketching rapidly. By the time I began painting around 11:00 P.M., the sky had already changed and all I had to work with were my memory and the sketch. I was finished with it by the first light of dawn.

David pointed out the heart in the sky and said, "Look, the point of the heart is coming from that ridge there. That's exactly where I was, sending you this message, with my heart full of love for you, knowing how those were your kind of clouds." I had painted this so rapidly in a sort of altered consciousness, I had not yet seen the heart myself.

PLATE 26. *Reading* Newsweek, *1989, oil, 32" x 36"*

MY HUSBAND, DAVID, WAS A "WATER-baby." He loved to soak in a tub. One of his favorite times for doing this was when *Newsweek* magazine arrived. He would pile up sticks and small logs under the old water heater, start a fire, and soon have enough hot water for a full tub. While waiting fifteen minutes or so for the water to heat, he would wash the soot from the globe of the kerosene lantern to ensure good reading light. Then David would sit in that tub and read the entire issue.

Other than the sink in the kitchen, there was no plumbing in the house. All the rest of the pipes were outside, and these were no more than what was needed for the showers and tub. We added a bathhouse later for indoor winter bathing, but for the first few years this was how it looked.

David had found an old water heater in the Alpine city dump. It still held water, so he ran PVC pipe to it, and by placing it on bricks, there was room to make a small fire underneath for heating. It took fifteen minutes for the hot fire of mesquite and desert willow to heat thirty gallons of water. When desert willow burns it smells just like Belogia perfume. That and the mesquite made a kind of incense for each bath.

The shower was right there too. It was just a PVC pipe that hung off the roof with a ball valve to turn it on. It all worked just fine. But when there was a wind out of the north, it got behind the down-flowing water and sprayed it way out in front. When trying to rinse the soap out of my hair, I would often have to run forward or backward, trying to stay under the water. To this day I prefer a down-flowing pour of water to the usual spray (minus the wind). It feels like a natural waterfall.

Now, on my present ranch in Bellville, I have a wonderful old-fashioned tub-and-shower setup outdoors behind a lattice of climbing vines. It is a spiritual experience to sit out there at night and sink deep under the bubbles of a warm ginger bath, listening to owls, frogs, and coyotes while watching the moon and stars.

It was pretty romantic out in the desert too. One night, a dating couple spending a week with us took a bottle of wine out to the tub in back. The next morning they told us that while in that tub, they had decided to get married.

THERE ARE MORE SPANISH DAGGER and century plants in Mexico than in the Texas Chihuahuan Desert. When century plants grow in a high altitude, they develop beautiful orange buds that open to yellow. The plant blooms only once, at the end of its life, which is actually about twenty years rather than one hundred. Before it blooms it sends out many daughter plants from its roots, and as it blooms, the heavy stiff leaves begin to age. They carry the scars of various injuries from hail, insects, and other encounters, including the permanent marks of its own blades' saw-toothed edges, imprinted when the plant was young and curled tightly against itself.

Nothing pollinates the century plant but bats. However, the nectar is available for the hummingbirds as well. Lizards love to bask on the blades, and knowing this, the roadrunner usually checks the century plant for its favorite food. In fact, the female roadrunner will not mate with the male unless he first brings her a lizard offering; if she accepts it, she accepts him. The males spend a lot of time watching out for lizards.

During the mating season, the roadrunner utters the most mournful lovesick call. We had several of these birds tamed around the house, and they loved the beef jerky we held out for them. We knew the male had a sweetheart when, instead of eating the jerky, he ran off swiftly, holding the jerky high like a trophy, and disappeared behind a bush.

We easily tamed roadrunners to take food from us, but one year a stalking rooster from our chicken house ran them off. This rooster was a terrible misfit. His crow was broken and it sounded horrible. It was some kind of

PLATE 27. *Century Plant in Bloom, 1996, oil, 72" x 34"*

squawking shrieking noise. He never could correct it. A rooster with a good crow is a beautiful thing to hear—a maestro who will yodel the last few notes and then hold them, long and sweet. I began to complain that this one needed to be done in before he created more of his kind with our hens.

David and Mark laughed and thought nothing of it. But this rooster must have kept getting banned from the henhouse. He soon began to lurk around my home, and damn it, he would see me and begin that horrendous ear-splitting shriek any time of day. I named him Jackson, and I would go outside to shoo him away, but he would just circle the house eyeing me. I could not believe it when he began stalking me. He would be outside the house if I was there, or if I was in my studio, the blasted rooster would show up there, standing up on tiptoes to peek in the window. Of course, if he saw me, he would inflict that diabolical scream on me and pace back and forth beneath the window.

I saw Jackson run at the roadrunner one morning, and after that the roadrunner stopped coming around. The other two roosters would mind their business and keep up with the hens; none of them crowed during the day except Jackson. He would wait until I was taking a nap and then sound off right beside the sleeping porch, screeching over and over again. The last time that rooster stalked me and began his racket outside my window, I picked up my Browning .22 rifle and shot him in the head.

A few days later my roadrunner returned.

Roadrunner

PLATE 28. *The Man Who Sleeps in Cactus, 1991, oil, 42" x 36"*

IN NEW MEXICO A MAN TOLD ME OF an Indian myth about the man who sleeps in cactus. He did not know too much about it, but the name started a painting for me. Most of the year people adapt to the desert heat by sleeping out of doors. So here is someone who has gone beyond adaptation.

The need to put in coyotes kept after me until I "obeyed"; that is when I realized the man is a trickster. However, as trickster, he teases and chides. "Why do you need to sleep on a mattress? What is the matter with you? See me, I just sleep here comfortably cradled by these spines."

In American Indian religions, the Trickster often teaches by playing a joke on and making a fool of someone. That way, one learns something.

I knew there was more to this, and it came to me that he is also symbolic for people who have numbed themselves, have no feelings, and scorn those who do. The Trickster wants to shame others for taking care of their own needs and not being like him. But when others copy him and are not true to themselves, it hurts.

This painting helps me realize the folly of twisting myself into a pretzel trying to get others' approval. It helps me affirm my own individuality.

PLATE 29. *The Mating Dance of the Yucca Moth, 1989, oil, 44" x 48"*

THIS WAS JUST GOING TO BE A PAEAN OF praise for the beauty of the desert at night, my favorite time. After I finished, though, I knew it was about much more.

I had noticed that a few nights each year would be filled with small, white yucca moths flying in clouds and drifts everywhere. Anyone who had to drive at night would have their car plastered with them.

Learning more, I discovered that if either the yucca or the moth were to die out, the other would also be doomed. Each species of yucca is fertilized by its own species of moth, and those moths lay their eggs only in the center of their own species of yucca flower.

In this painting, the moths emerge one night, triggered by the same timing that opens the yucca flowers. Suddenly for a few nights the desert is filled with them. They fly in joy, mating in their own ecstasy. I painted the moths and stars mixing into the Milky Way, the edge of our galaxy, to remind us of the interrelatedness of all things in the universe. It is impossible to tell where the moths end and the stars begin.

From the smallest bug or the smallest plants, from the winged and the four-legged to humans, all things in this universe are interdependent in more ways than we may ever know. It fills me with deep wonder to contemplate how everything on the Earth came from star matter and that every living thing carries DNA just like humans. That mystery is like a good sermon on a Sunday morning.

PLATE 30.
*Canopus in
Winter Sky,
1994, oil,
34" x 28"*

I lie awake in my bedroll

on hard desert ground,

floating, unable to sleep for stars,

for the joy of looking and listening.

Owls known by their special voices,

coyotes loved for their songs,

creatures scurry about in chino grass.

At last overcome by sleep,

will someone please turn off the moon?

OH, SUMMER! MOST OF THE YEAR WAS
warm with cool to very cold nights. But when April
arrived, there would be a night or two to warn of the
trying times on the way. I rated nights by how soon the
evening chill made me reach for a sheet; in early summer
it delayed until four in the morning. Soon the only
coolness at all arrived at 7:30 A.M., the slight chill chased
down by the rising sun from the peaks to the valley,
coming from the ring of mountains that circled our
ranch. Then I would fall into blissful sleep only to have
the sun burst upon the bed with such ferocity by 8:30 or
9:00 A.M., the first rays burnt my skin as they touched
me; so much for sleeping late.

One strategy I soon learned for keeping cool, no
kidding, was walking out to the shower to stand while it
drenched my clothes and me. In the dry air the rapid
evaporation was always cooling; it only took thirty
minutes for my blue jeans to dry. Other times I used
spray bottles filled with water and kept nearby to cool off.
That was the trick at night, except I would be so suddenly chilled that I would gasp, and then in a few
minutes the dry air had me sweating again. Yes, you do
sweat in the desert, although you seldom realize how
much since it evaporates immediately. But the poor bed
would get soaked quickly, and we would have to roll
over to a new dry place. I was usually exhausted during
the hot summers, barely sleeping through the nights.
Days were even hotter and naps were impossible. I
usually returned to Houston during that time for a visit.
It may be hot and muggy in the city, but its buildings
have air conditioning!

The dogs had a large tub in the shade, half filled with
water, and they would take turns laying in it. My dog
would sit in the water and half close her eyes in blessed
relief. I have a dog tub in Houston, and in the city my
dog never wants to get wet. She learned it only makes
her hotter to have fur plastered against her body in 90
percent humidity.

At night I would lay on my side, cooler because
there is less body against the mattress, and stare out at the
sky. I could mark the path of the stars through the night
by watching them pass behind a porch post and re-
emerge. I had an eight-inch telescope and spent hours
looking at objects like the nebula in Orion, the Beehive,
the double star in Cygnus, and distant galaxies; most of
all I loved knowing the constellations. Soon I learned
that the width of my fist outstretched at arm's length was
equal to a twenty-degree measurement in the sky. I
could see where Aquila was at say 9:00 P.M., and then the
next night I could spot Aquila and tell that by its position

that the time was 11:00 P.M. With practice I could wake up in the middle of the night and know the time by looking at the sky. I also learned the phases of the moon and could use it to tell the time of night. We planned late-night horseback rides knowing when the moon would rise early, using it thereafter as our guide.

In the winter I would watch for enormous Canopus to rise in the center of the southern sky and skirt the tops of the mountains before setting. The thicker air on the horizon broke the bright light of that star into all the colors of the spectrum, sending shimmering streamers in all directions. Many of my visitors were convinced that it was really the flashing neon lights of a shopping mall in Mexico.

The night became one of my most beloved times. The hard desert becomes soft and seductive, blue-white in moonlight. I often walked outside barefoot, using only starlight or moonlight to see as I wandered around the yard listening to the burrowing owl, or the elf owl, or the great horned owl. If there had been a rain, the toads crawled up out of their burrows in the earth and began to croak, sounding like calves in distress. They would sing their hearts out for a night or two, then everything would dry up and the night silence returned.

Chapter 4
LETTING GO

Kerosene lantern sitting on dining room

table.

West wind blowing through cracks in the

adobe wall.

My lantern sputters, sometimes sizzles.

My marriage sometimes sizzles, often

sputters.

If that crack is not soon mended, they will

both go out.

WE HAD NO PHONE AT FRESNO RANCH, and the outlaw phone company wanted thirty-five thousand dollars to put in one for us. So, we built a bench and table by the pay phone in Lajitas at the corner of the motel, and I sat there with starving-at-the-phone food for hours making the calls I needed for business, to family, or to friends. The six-mile drive to the phone was an awful nuisance. I had to remember to bring bank statements, bills, water, and a hat and coats for sudden cold weather with each trip. Lots of times Mexicans or tourists clustered near me, as if in line. I thought they were eavesdropping and would tell them where other phones were in Lajitas, but that would not always encourage them to move off. If the call was really private, I might have to leave and give my turn to the people "in line," hoping when I came back I would be alone again.

When the dust storms, or maybe just a dust devil, whipped up suddenly, I would double over to shield my face, saying to the person on the phone "Just a minute," then try to continue the conversation, usually with a mouthful of dust despite my efforts, when the wind settled. If people were "out for a minute" when I called,

I would have to think of something to do while I waited to try again: call someone else, perhaps go into town to Frontier Drugstore for a turkey-pastrami on rye and a Dr. Pepper. The pay phone's ring had been silenced, probably because it would bother tourists using the bedroom next door, so it was nearly impossible to have someone call me back; I would have to be a psychic to know when to pick up the silent phone. (Well, O.K., I am kind of psychic, but not that good.)

After many years, I learned at last that my congressman could help. I called the office of Lloyd Bentson, and I was told that the Rural Electrification Act gave us a right to have a phone installed. Moreover, they had recently funded our phone company with over twenty million dollars, and the congressman's staff implied that they were outraged to hear that the company wanted to charge us. A very sheepish phone official drove out to see us not long after that, climbing slowly out of his car after pulling up to our house. "Seems like y'all 'er gonna be getting a phone." I wanted to shout something back in gleeful spite but remained composed and invited him in for cold water. By this time I had been at Fresno Ranch for ten years. David and I finally got phone lines not only to our house but also to every building that needed a phone.

The phone went in the month after I left for Houston to receive treatment for cancer. My marriage deteriorated so horribly over arguments about what kind of treatment I should seek that I had to send David back to Fresno Ranch just to continue my treatments with some hope of healing.

He believed I was contaminated, declaring he could feel the radiation treatments emanating from me, and did not want to kiss me because it made him squeamish. I began divorce proceedings the next year. I never returned to live at Fresno Ranch and only got to use that phone many years later, after the ranch reverted to me.

I would not live my life any differently if I had the chance. David was a lot of fun, although his brother Mark held the ranch together. I could not comprehend the red-flag warnings about David all around me. Our relationship problem was like the catfish in the slough: big, obvious, and in plain sight. Both Mark and I were besotted with David and his declarations of spirituality. He often said he was "but a tourist visiting civilization," pausing to add, "and my head is in the clouds." Mark had grown up adoring and respecting his older brother, and I came under David's charming spell and believed his words too.

Are you wondering what became of the "knowing" experience I had with the name Sleeper and the message I thought I understood? It is so mysterious the way things work out. I think it was right while being wrong. Let me explain.

All those years at Fresno Ranch I learned invaluable things about the desert, about ranching, and about myself. Also, I grew to know, respect, and love Mark and his wife, Gretta.

It just so happened that when I knew I had to end the marriage, Mark and Gretta were ready to move on as well. Today, they manage my ranch, Bend N Creek, in Bellville, where we all three live. They are beloved family, not to mention excellent ranchers. *So, it was and is a Sleeper for life!*

I BOUGHT A CUTE LITTLE FOUR-WHEELER I called Tortuga and began using it instead of a horse. It was nice not to have to go out, find it, and catch it before riding. I would use it to scoot about in the desert or to get down to the river's side quickly, and my husband, brother-in-law Mark, and I took it on wild runs down arroyos and up and down clay hills.

One day, as I rode down a steep road on the ranch, the hand accelerator jammed in full throttle, and I was headed for a stone building. Recent rain had created deep ruts, and I plowed across these perpendicularly, going airborne as I tried putting on the brakes. Braking and turning did not stop my forward course, and I crashed sideways into the stone porch wall. I fell onto the porch, through the screen, back out again, and onto the ground. The crash broke seven ribs, a collarbone, and punctured a lung. All I could say was "awh . . . oh . . . awh," too stunned to feel pain.

I was rushed to Alpine by the Terlingua medics, and after a tube was shoved into my side, I went on a machine that kept my lung inflated. A week later I moved to a friend's house in Alpine to recuperate, with help, before the one-hundred-mile drive home. Hal and Mary Flanders and their wonderful daughter, Beth Ann, a nurse, took care of me until I could safely return to the ranch down on the river.

As the universe tends to provide, a shaman from Bolivia named Isabel passed through Alpine just as I left the hospital. A friend, Feather, knew her very well and brought her to me. Isabel offered to perform a healing she had learned from Indians in the depths of the Bolivian jungles. I asked her what beliefs were behind her work.

She explained that she had to call on the spirits to restore to me my little "piece of spirit" that broke off during the accident and remained behind. Isabel added

Longhorns —
Noteworthy '93 Rancho Picachos

PLATE 31. *Shaman Summoning My Broken Spirit, 1987, oil, 36" x 48"*

that if I passed by the accident site and called to it, the broken piece of spirit might return to me. However, she thought this unlikely since it would be so injured as to be too frightened to move from where it fell. Without it, she said, healing would be slow, incomplete, and unsatisfactory. I was curious, and dubious, but agreed, trying to remain open minded.

Isabel prepared me for the ritual late one night in my room at the Flanders. She told me to protect myself from evil spirits and from wandering spirits, for when she summoned the Spirit World many would arrive. To help in this she gave me a small obsidian cross to wear around my neck. The black, she said, would absorb any evil and keep me safe. She made everyone leave the room, turned off the light, and began chanting in the dark. I could see her by dim light, turning slowly and holding out the shirt I had been wearing, murmuring softly until at last she said: "Ees very far away. Ees no wan' to come."

I begged, "Oh, don't give up. It is very far away. Over a hundred miles." A narrow beam of light came through the window from the street, and I watched her anxiously: more chanting and circling, holding, dancing the shirt like a bullfighter's cape, and cajoling of the spirit. At last, she suddenly caught the little spirit in the shirt and wrapped it up and laid the bundle on my chest. She then left in silence. I was to remain quiet until the next day in order to prevent scaring away the tender, frightened piece of my spirit.

This experience proved to be very moving, despite my skepticism. The little bundle of my shirt and the tiny spirit laid on my chest was like the new bundle placed on my chest after delivering a baby. I felt the thrill of being reunited in a special way. I thought to myself, "If one's psychology has anything to do with healing, then this ceremony surely has put me in the right frame of mind."

As it turned out, I healed more rapidly than the specialist expected. The brace for the collarbone crushed my broken ribs, so I could not use that device. Every time I bent over to put on shoes, the collarbone fell forward and apart. I learned to hold it with my hand if I had to bend over. It is stunning how many tasks require bending over! Yet the collarbone healed without any lump. The muscles in my painting arm had been unusable for two months, but then suddenly became strong and pain free; in joy and reverence I created this painting as soon as I was well.

We know that to relieve the burden of a trauma, we must revisit the scene with a guide, either in actuality or in therapy. One goal is to be restored to one's former self. Some truths that seem to us to be newly *discovered* are only newly *uncovered*. This painting speaks of the value of ceremony, whether ancient or spontaneous. We are physical beings, and it seems important to me to let the body be involved in its fullest way.

The scene depicted here is from my Rancho Picachos. I placed Isabel, the Bolivian, south of the Rio Grande but overlooking Fresno Ranch; we call that cliff Shaman Peak now. The Chisos Mountains are in the far distance.

To achieve the glow on the nearby mountains from the late sun cutting through clouds, I used many layers of color. Halfway through I laid on a transparent black that I mix, using a four-inch housepainter's brush, then painted the final brilliant golds into the black, producing effects impossible to achieve any other way. There is something about the irony, if you will, or the spiritual truth contained in the fact that covering up parts with a brush dipped into black helped bring out the golden luminosity that radiates from this work. The well of our joy is dug by our pain.

PLATE 32. *Northern
Lights, 1989, oil, 56" x 40"*

Big Bend is a land where

Mountains stretch

To touch the sky

Ever out of reach.

Big Bend goes up and up

Through the clouds

Past the stars

And beyond.

I HAD ONLY A SHORT WAVE RADIO, AND spent many painting hours listening to Armed Forces Radio, the BBC, Australia, and other stations around the world. Then one day, the radio went dead, except for a cyclic buzzing. The screen said "error." I went to my back-up radio. Same problem. Horrors, had Europe been bombed? All day I tried and could not get any station, not even Cuba, which seemed to blast itself across many locations on the airwaves.

That night there was a very red sunset, which never disappeared. It hung pulsing in the sky, from west to east, across the entire northern sky. There appeared sporadic, thin columns of white, and then just as suddenly they were gone. There might be three or five or none. The pulsing red glow made David suspect it was a fire. A rock fire? Impossible . . . and this seemed to come from miles away. But it did pulse like the glow from a fire. All night it grew stronger, then softer, then stronger, then softer. I would never have guessed it was the northern lights this far south. I had seen the aurora borealis in Wisconsin when I went to Camp Nagawicka as a girl. I had been told that Wisconsin was almost too far south for such a display. You could not see it every night, and when you did, it was very pale green or pale blue, and you had to strain to see it, distinct from the Milky Way.

The next day I learned from my friends who had TVs that there had been a huge solar flare, causing radios to go out and colors in the sky. Later, I got my *Science News Weekly* and read that the solar flare had been as long as thirty earths, the longest in recorded history. The northern lights had been seen as far south as Puerto Rico! We saw it for two more nights, and then again the next year, almost to the day, in March, but quite diminished.

I was so grateful to have had the chance to see that, especially with no knowledge of what it was, just like the aboriginal people. I had the chance to marvel at the mysteries of the universe in a fresh way, which was denied folks who lived in the center of city lights and had received advance warning. I gained a fresh appreciation of the development of old religions, superstitions, and the strange rules adopted by tribes. I certainly had a long day and night to understand the sovereignty of nature, and how so many of our religions have traditions that trace back to the earliest times, when God, not science, ruled.

IN THE HARSH DESERT, ALL THINGS MUST seek ways to protect and isolate themselves from the burning sun. They find ways to wall themselves off from scalding heat with wax, thorns, or hard shells to protect their vital remaining liquid from being sucked dry by wind or predators. Thirsty animals use the cactus as a source of water. Even humans remember it can save their life if stranded.

The cactus is the only source of water in this painting. Even the clouds in the sky are moving elsewhere. If ever they gather to rain, it will not be here this day.

There are people who are tragically and beautifully vulnerable and surround themselves with hostilities that prevent approach. The relatively barren landscape is symbolic of those who are deprived of spiritual waters that would enable them to grow safely without spiny protection. In this painting the air holds almost no humidity, and any rain that falls evaporates before it hits the ground.

I have loved persons who have a deep well of spirituality within, but fearing their own vulnerability, they struggle to protect themselves. Like the cactus they wound me, friends and foes alike; they will eventually live very much alone in the desert of their own making.

In the cactus shadow rests a rattlesnake, taking advantage of the only shade in a vast space. There have been loved ones in my life who, because of their lifestyle, sheltered something deadly in their shadow, dangerous should anyone come too close.

One aspect of my recovery is learning to discern those who can only hurt me. I can love them, but I must part with them. Another is understanding that saying "No" to them is saying "Yes" to me.

PLATE 33. *Cactus and Cloud Streets, 1985, oil, 38" x 44"*

I TOOK A FIVE-DAY FLOAT TRIP DOWN
the Rio Grande with five other women. One was a
shaman who had been trained in North Texas. One
evening she led us in a shamanic journey. We made a
circle of stones and placed to the south one lechuguilla
stalk tied with two raven feathers we found. We were
told to take notice of which direction we chose to sit in,
or chose to face, for that held meaning for this stage of
our life. Each direction contains its own wisdom and
guidance. We were going to do some sort of soul searching called "finding a circle of self."

It was a powerful evening for all of us. To hypnotic
drumming we went on an inward journey to see what or
who was waiting for us with a message. Our shaman
guide took us to the Upper World. She said that trained
shamans visit the Lower World, but it can be treacherous
and the return difficult. Since we were all new to this, we
took a safer journey.

The next morning I went back to visit the site. I
noticed that there were faces in all the cliff walls. I
thought they were only due to the morning light, but
when I returned that afternoon, the same faces were
there. I noticed that a number of them resembled aged
Indian women and men. It was like they had come out
of the wall to witness a circle of which they approved.

During the passing of a few months, I heard other
river guides tell of taking their raft of tourists to that
canyon and how not one of them ever dislodged a stone
or the lechuguilla stalk, commenting rather about how
special it felt there, walking carefully past the circle.
Anyone who knows the usual crowd of tourists knows
there are at least one vandal and one scoffer in any
nonselect group. The guides were in awe of the respect
the tourists consistently showed.

Then the show was over. A heavy rain flooded the
canyon and washed new stones down, filling the canyon
floor with more than ten feet of water. The flood was so
deep that gravel covered up the hanging stone, which is
in the gap in the canyon walls, beginning about six feet
high. Now we know it could be centuries before the
next rain happens in just the right way to uncover that
spot. The circle, the stalk, and the raven feathers will
remain in place much longer than we expected.

The canyons and *tinajas* behave just like the way I
paint. They cover up, then uncover. One can walk
through a canyon, treacherously clinging to slippery rock
around a deep *tinaja* of black water, and on the next visit
walk in on a flat gravel surface with no sign of the *tinaja*.
This might make someone feel lost and bewildered.
Most folk are unaware of the vast scale of nature's play.
The visitor will think he or she is in the wrong canyon
or has not gone far enough. Unless one has a topo-
graphical map or knows some special shapes on the
canyon walls, it all may remain a mystery.

I waited two years to paint this, and the knowledge
that the original site is now covered up is as much the
impetus to paint it as what occurred there.

One morning I began sketching. The power animals
of the Chihuahuan Desert and the spiny plants that grow
there kept popping up in the sketches. I walked away to
sit on the porch and listen to the wind chimes. When I
returned I saw at once that these images wanted to be
part of the painting.

Suddenly it all fell into place. The outermost edge is
a line of textured gold leaf over the oil paint, the spiny
plants arranged as guardians around the perimeter. Next
the power animals, beginning with coyote and the
trickster, move up the sides, increasing in rank to the
eagle. A numinous figure stands to either side, each with
an escort animal. The moon has a rabbit, for in these

parts they do not see the "man in the moon" but the "rabbit in the moon." Knowing this, can you see the rabbit in the full moon?

For me, this painting is an icon of the strength of other paths and other beliefs, the healing that is available for all of us when we stay open to what life brings to us.

PLATE 34. *The Shaman's Circle of Self, 1990, oil, 48" x 36"*

PLATE 35. *The West Door,*
1989, oil, 42" x 60"

LATE ONE NIGHT, I SAW A DOOR IN THE west sky, framed by stars. There was a lovely, pale-blue transparency there, like a rectangular opening in the sky—as if the sky had thinned and was letting light from Heaven shine through. I thought to myself, "Hmmm, I think that's the door I'll go through when I die." There was something reassuring about it, and it was as if I had been given a comforting glimpse of another dimension.

To see what stars had formed that "door," I looked at my large stellar map and discovered that it was the constellation Pisces, which was setting in the west. Pisces is the last constellation of the twelve, the end. It is also the edge of the new beginning, which arrives next with Aries in spring. It gives further depth to the meaning of ending, of dying, of being reborn, ending only to begin again, giving up a phase to begin a new one.

The cause of the glow eluded me for several years, because no town was in that part of the horizon. Ojinaga and Presidio were farther to the north. The sun had set four hours earlier. This puzzled me for some time. At last, I saw a similar glow like this just as a late-setting sickle moon dropped behind Poster Peak. Understanding the cause did not ruin it for me at all, for a spiritual experience does not depend on being ignorant of the laws of nature. Instead, for me, a thing as simple as a sunset can suddenly envelop me as an embrace in the arms of God.

The idea of a door to another world is also in another painting, *Carlotta Tinaja,* in which there is a reflection of a tunnel in the water. In both of these works, the existence of a prepared door, or a special tunnel, implies the existence of another room, another cave, another world, where exploration and life occur in ways not clear on this side. Perhaps one cannot return after entering this new dimension.

Reality is no more than that which is real to each of us. To have a magical moment explained by hard science does not detract from the significance for me, for all things work together to produce truth. This experience helped me dispel the fear of the unknown, the future, and most of all, my own ending.

PLATE 36. *Releasing My Eagles, 1991, oil, 39" x 54"*

AS I UNDERWENT WRENCHING CHANGES in my life, I wanted some way to say how hard it is to let go, how necessary it is for growth but how painful.

I was losing the man I thought I would love for the rest of my life, someone who I thought was going to always love me. I was losing my marriage, my ranch I called home for ten years, and the ability to live in the desert that fed my soul. I had lost my left breast. I had lost my long hair, going bald with chemotherapy, and I might even soon lose my life.

I had to paint this picture to help cope with all the horror I was experiencing. The path on the right is where I had worn a trail coming down daily to keep those eagles in the pen. The eagles are very mature, having been in captivity many years. They are my expectations and cherished illusions. I have removed my sandals because this "letting go" is a spiritual act and the ground there is holy. Using the four directions, I have created a sacred circle of prayer stones.

Whenever you see a golden key, you know you are in the presence of myth. A myth is not something of fantasy but something that contains universal truths. When I opened the cage, the eagles were weak from years of captivity, so they push off against me, cutting me badly. However you do it, letting go hurts.

The storm in the background is no longer over me, but the gales from it still buffet me on the mountaintop. Keeping the attachment to delusions and illusions that are unhealthy is like moving through a rock outcrop: by doing it long enough, one will make a trail through the things that were once impediments. As I release my illusions in emotional turmoil, the storm moves across my awareness, yet not over me, no longer hindering me.

The act of letting go, of profoundly saying goodbye from the depths of one's soul and releasing one's grasp totally, is not possible without strong spiritual help.

PLATE 37. *The Spirit of the Rio Grande, 1990, oil, 52" x 38"*

I WAS IN HOUSTON UNDERGOING treatment for breast cancer. At the time I thought I was painting this out of a longing for my home in Big Bend. I centered the river so the viewer stands straddling the shores of Mexico on the left and Texas on the right, a view I saw every day as I drove toward my ranch from Lajitas.

A mountain that commands the western horizon from my ranch has been a subject I have returned to repeatedly. It was formed from hundreds of feet of volcanic ash and has several caps of different lava. It has faulted, and a part has dropped down to the left. I have grown to love that mountain. The entry gate to my ranch perfectly frames it as I turn to drive in. The sight of that mountain said to me, "You are home."

I thought the painted clouds took on their swirling shape because I was unconsciously describing the spiritual energy that mountain gives me. Now I know that is only the tip of the iceberg. It is also my breast, once flowing with milk for each of my six children, now lopped off. The loss of my breast is a source of spiritual energy, nonetheless, for it propelled me into ever-deeper searches for truth and healing.

I cannot say today that I totally regret that cancer, for it has given an increased dimension to my life, as have my years in the desert. Straddling the river of life, I also faced up to the end of my marriage.

For two years after that painting, I continued to stand in the center of the river, the center of not knowing. I did not know if after the divorce I would return to the desert. I could not even be sure if I would still be healthy enough to want to. But I could not begin to imagine living anywhere else. Regardless of where I might end up living, I could still look up to the Great Spirit that holds all of us in his hands and trust that whatever worked out was right for me.

I WAS THRILLED TO RETURN TO MY home in Big Bend for a few weeks' visit after nine months of doctors in Houston. My sister-in-law, Gretta, said she was saving a surprise for me.

One spring, after a lot of good rain, we rode to a place beside the Rio Grande. There before us was a huge field of white poppies. They were tall and elegant, and their tissue-thin crinkled petals fluttered in the breeze like butterfly wings.

I was utterly delighted! I got off my horse and crouched down amongst them, looking at the patterns of sunlight coming through their petals. Gretta knew me well. This was a treat.

I merely intended to paint them, with no other meaning than "Look! How lovely!" But, because of what I was going through and learning, painfully, this work reads like pages of my diary.

The poppies celebrate the serenity that soars free and high once one has begun to detach and let go of parts of one's life that are changing or leaving anyway. It shows how a flower, rooted to one place, can detach itself and fly free, transforming itself. If the poppies can do it, maybe I can too.

There is life after cancer. I painted the poppies, flying like birds, changing shapes joyously in their dance.

PLATE 38. *Detaching: Flight of the Poppies #2, 1992, oil, 36" x 41"*

Living alone.
> *Isolated.*
> *No possibility of TV.*
> *No phone.*
> *Just silence.*

No trees to catch the sound of the wind.
> *Dust devils churn by, flinging drawings to the*
> > *ground.*
> *A lizard with orange sides and turquoise belly*
> *darts past.*
> *I do not see his belly,*
> *but I know of it, nonetheless.*

Sitting on a boulder beside the creek,
> *my bare toes play with pebbles in the water,*
> *and I shrink to live in one of the braided*
> *streams of Fresno Creek.*

I glance at the northern horizon
> *and slide up and down the flatirons of the*
> > *Solitario.*
> *I notice the Lower Shutup and travel*
> *through that narrow canyon*
> *to the inner sanctum of circling limestone*
> *and fields of colored rocks,*
> *black, red, green.*

So I continue to live within myself,
> *flattened out for miles under the sun*
> *and spreading, blown, huge, round, globe-like,*
> *throughout the sky in all directions. I am.*
> *Large and at once present,*
> *here, there, and everywhere.*

I glance behind me to the east,
> *and see the setting sun paint Castle Rock*
> *brilliant gold and orange, and I am up there*
> *400 feet higher, braced*
> *against the stronger winds of day's end.*

From the highest peak
> *I look at the delta of Fresno Creek,*
> *how it trickles beneath sand and gravel,*
> *spreading out at the Rio Grande,*
> *joining that Mother River*
> *in her riotous rapids.*

I return to the creek to walk on.
> *Small, insignificant as a frog,*
> *I have no impact here.*
> *I am welcome here,*
> *. . . I belong.*

This place that accepts me
> *would not notice if I left.*
> *Only I would know.*
> *There is relief in that.*
> *The pressure is off.*
> *I am free.*

In some parts of the world those high cirrus clouds
> *foretell a change in the weather, but I know here*
> *they foretell All of Autumn.*
> *The change is lazy.*

Clouds adrift in streamers and chrysanthemum bursts
> *accompanied by patterns of buttermilk sky.*
> *Often UFO clouds form on the lee side of*
> > *mountains,*

pancake saucer clouds.
The days pass by thus.

I am no longer curious to hear a weather report.
Need a rock report?
A mountain report?
All things just are.

Like the stones, the sand, the creosote bushes,
I live in the desert, walk in the weather,
sleep in the weather, exist in the weather.

My ties to the earth become visible.
I chose my clothes not for fashion
but for the earth that I walk upon,
for the sun, for the wind.

My long hair is a barometer:
down, russet streaming over
my shoulders, it is cool today.
Pony tail, it is a pleasant day.
Wound up high, it is hot as hell.
So I have summer hats, a size bigger,
to fit over all that pinned up hair.

Feet softened by August
become callused by March.
The scalding desert ground
requires shoes in the summer.

A loner who lived in a hole in the ground.
Not that different from some of my friends
who moved into roofless adobes in the Ghost
*   Town*
and cheerfully called it home.

Many, if not all my friends
in Study Butte, Terlingua, Lajitas,
are loners of some kind. We get together
for nights of music by talented locals,
children out on the floor, dancing,
maybe some barbecue, always beer.
Then we drift back into our private lives.

New music is composed, becomes popular in the States
and disappears. Movies flood the theaters
and are gone. TV serials arrive and thrill the
*   citizenry*
for several years, then leave.
Newsweek comes without fail
and mentions these things.

I begin to wonder about the unseen world beyond my
*   desert.*
The thick, swarming coils of entangled human
*   encounters*
that I have remembered with distaste.
That I now remember with compassion.

I peek through my fingers and begin to see the people.
I am healing.

My profound connection to earth has restored me
to my disowned society of others.
There on the freeways, they are also me,
and now, also here, with me.
But out here where I can barely be found,
I am more connected than ever before.

Now I see in my mind the cities, the houses,
the rooms I have visited,

lived in, fought in, cried in,
and I am there
while I stand in the wide rocky driveway,
in the cool of deep summer evening,
listening to owls.

Under more stars than we ever imagined,
I walk by starlight
and see my shadow
cast by the light of Venus
as she sets in the west.

Benign vastness holds me in its hand,
reconnects me to all the unseen
known, unknown and forgotten,
the loved and the despised,
the dangerous and the boring.

"She always was strange," they said,
and then forgot me.

It's O.K. now.
Their opinions, like the varied colors
of the painted bunting and the gray junco,
are just who they are,
like who I am.
Their behavior fits them,
like frogs hop, lizards dart, and falcons dive.

Frogs don't like snakes,
snakes fear red-tailed hawks,
and coyotes love mice.

Would I want all species to bark like dogs?
Do I not prefer other people
to be truly other?
As even I
am now truly me.

EPILOGUE

LIKE EVERYONE WHO RECEIVED THE call in December 1998, I did not want to believe that death had finally caught up with Jeanne Norsworthy. She had dodged its insidious tentacles with her plucky determination so many times, I had come to consider her invincible.

Yet I was not surprised, for Jeanne Norsworthy had let go of so many things in her life. By so doing, she had already moved into a spiritual realm that allowed her remarkable insights into her past, present, and future. It is a space that few of us ever experience, much less write about.

In the summer of 1998, when she asked me to help edit the text for this book, I agreed to read what had already been written. I was on a plane to some-where, and before I knew it, several hours had literally flown by and we were landing. There was no doubt in my mind that I wanted to be a part of Jeanne's effort, because it meant I would get to know this woman whose powers of seeing and translating her vision into paints were nothing short of exceptional.

Exceptional is the word that best describes Jeanne.

Physically, she was exceptionally beautiful, radiating a karmic *joie de vivre* that found a place in all of her paintings. Despite the fact that she had lost her hair through chemotherapy and that her organs had been burned and her flesh punctured, laughter permeated just about everything she said, much of which was aimed at herself. "Will this be of interest to anybody?" she would ask me as we arranged the visuals and stories that go with them. "Yes, yes it will," I assured her repeatedly.

Jeanne's life was poetry, and when she talked about it in slide lectures or wrote about it, the words poured out like the paints on her canvases, expressing emotions that even she did not understand until she had worked through the process. When Jeanne turned to reflect on what she had said, written, or painted, however, she isolated the elements, and like a shaman's ritual, the pattern of their arrangement brought about deeper revelations.

At the time, I was going through a divorce myself and was getting ready to exit the same posh neighbor-hood that Jeanne had forsaken decades earlier. Perhaps I was drawn to her parables like an acolyte in search of guru. Whatever brought us together, her message to me was clear: Always pour as much of yourself into what you are doing as you can afford to, and then pour a little bit more. Whether it is raising children, making a painting, saving a ranch, meeting new people, loving a man, loving yourself, finding a cure for your ailments, or absorbing the healing elements of nature, do it as if there is no tomorrow.

Jeanne knew this truism all her life. Her urgency to share it before her demise rings in every word of her text.

—*Susan Hallsten McGarry*

Jeanne Norsworthy

1935–1998

ISBN 1-58544-140-6